"In her book *How Would Buddha Act?*, Barbara Kipfer, PhD, offers the reader many diverse and practical means to translate ancient wisdom teachings into positive action in today's world. Students of the Buddha's teachings will likely feel quite at home with the teachings, essays, and meditations in this book, and should enjoy the author's suggestions to bring those forward in the busyness of modern life. Readers not so familiar with Buddhist teachings will nonetheless benefit from reading and practicing any of these meditations, because, ultimately, these teachings and meditations, just like the teachings of the Buddha, are pointing us to always-present possibilities and direct methods for experiencing our lives with great wonder, and in ways that are at once deeply human and profoundly beautiful."

—**Jeff Brantley, MD**, assistant consulting professor in the department of psychiatry and behavioral sciences at Duke University Medical Center; founding faculty member of Duke Integrative Medicine, and founder and director of its mindfulness-based stress reduction (MBSR) program; Distinguished Life Fellow of the American Psychiatric Association; author of *Calming Your Angry Mind*; and coauthor of *Daily Meditations for Calming Your Angry Mind*

"Books on mindfulness are plentiful, yet those with an emphasis on ethics are in short supply. Mindfulness without an understanding of the deeper problems of greed and aversion can become self-serving. *How Would Buddha Act?* is a welcome exception. From its *Dhammapada*-like sayings to its practical guidance for dealing with strong emotions to its guided meditations, this book can be a helpful companion for living an ethical life."

—**Arnie Kozak, PhD**, author of *The Awakened Introvert* and *Mindfulness A to Z*

"In our stressful, overbooked lives, it's all too easy to move through our days on autopilot—overdoing everything from eating and drinking to shopping, watching TV, and surfing the Internet. In this wise and engaging guide to the Buddhist concept of Right Action, Barbara Ann Kipfer offers a diverse array of teachings, meditations, and essays designed to help us act more skillfully and more lovingly to others and—ultimately—to ourselves."

—**Carol Krucoff, E-RYT**, yoga therapist at Duke Integrative Medicine, and author of several books, including *Yoga Sparks* and *Healing Yoga for Neck and Shoulder Pain* (www.healingmoves.com)

"A fun book that is full of wisdom as well. Because it can be read in short sections, *How Would Buddha Act?* will be especially helpful for anyone who wants a lively way to take in reminders about mindfulness practice."

—**Sharon Salzberg**, author of *Lovingkindness* and *Real Happiness*

"Open to any page in *How Would Buddha Act?* and you will find inspiration and practical support you can apply throughout your day. Presented in a friendly, accessible style, Barbara Ann Kipfer offers skillful guidance for living in a way that creates more happiness and well-being for others and yourself."

—**Richard Shankman**, author of *The Art and Skill of Buddhist Meditation*, and cofounder of Mindful Schools

"We all feel frustrated when we notice our actions taking a wrong turn and leaving our beliefs behind, and when we judge those around us for acting as if they've forgotten what really matters in life. Open *How Would Buddha Act?* to any page and find the right inspiration to nudge your actions back onto the path of your own wise heart."

—**Kimber Simpkins**, author of *Full* and *52 Ways to Love Your Body*

The **FOLLOWING BUDDHA** Series

Based on the teachings of the Eightfold Path, the *Following Buddha* series offers ancient wisdom to help you thrive in the modern world. Designed for both the avid Buddhist and the casual reader alike, these fun and accessible books provide thousands of teachings and affirmations to help you navigate all aspects of life—from building meaningful relationships, to balancing work and home life, to simply choosing one's words wisely.

If you want to act, think, or speak more like Buddha would, the enlightening books in this series will be your go-to guides.

• • •

**Visit www.followingbuddha.com
for more books in this series.**

how would would buddha act?

801 Right-Action Teachings
for Living with Awareness and Intention

• • •

BARBARA ANN KIPFER, PhD

New Harbinger Publications, Inc.

Publisher's Note

This publication is designed to provide accurate and authoritative information in regard to the subject matter covered. It is sold with the understanding that the publisher is not engaged in rendering psychological, financial, legal, or other professional services. If expert assistance or counseling is needed, the services of a competent professional should be sought.

Distributed in Canada by Raincoast Books

Copyright © 2016 by Barbara Ann Kipfer
          New Harbinger Publications, Inc.
          5674 Shattuck Avenue
          Oakland, CA 94609
          www.newharbinger.com

Cover design by Debbie Berne; Text design by Michele Waters-Kermes; Acquired by Melissa Valentine; Edited by James Lainsbury

Library of Congress Cataloging-in-Publication Data

Kipfer, Barbara Ann.
  How would Buddha act? : 801 right-action teachings for living with awareness and intention6 / Barbara Ann Kipfer, PhD.
    pages cm. -- (The new harbinger following Buddha series)
  ISBN 978-1-62625-312-4 (pbk. : alk. paper) -- ISBN 978-1-62625-313-1 (pdf e-book) -- ISBN 978-1-62625-314-8 (epub) 1. Religious life--Buddhism. I. Title.
  BQ5405.K57 2016
  294.3'444--dc23
                2015028420

MIX
Paper from
responsible sources
FSC® C011935
www.fsc.org

Printed in the United States of America

18   17   16

10 9 8 7 6 5 4 3 2 1   First printing

Thank you to New Harbinger for the opportunity to present this material. Great thanks to my editor and husband, Paul Magoulas, who inspires me to practice more Right Action in my life.

Thank you to everyone who supports my efforts to convey what I have learned, especially my sons Kyle Kipfer and Keir Magoulas.

—Barbara Ann Kipfer

Contents

Introduction

Think about how you get yourself in trouble by reacting instead of responding. The focus of *How Would Buddha Act?* is on training yourself to understand that you don't "get away with" anything; every thought, word, and deed has a consequence. A lot of what goes wrong in our lives is caused by not understanding the consequences of our actions.

Right Action is one of the elements in Buddha's Noble Eightfold Path to enlightenment. The path's elements are Right Speech, Right Action, Right View, Right Intention or Thought, Right Livelihood, Right Effort, Right Mindfulness, and Right Concentration.

What is Right Action? In simple terms, it is doing no harm. The Buddha specifically said that Right Action includes Five Precepts: abstaining from killing or harming living beings, refraining from taking what is not given freely, not committing sexual misconduct, not misusing intoxicants, and not using harmful speech. You can see that these words translate into "doing no harm." If you act in loving, compassionate ways, responding with the intention of doing no harm and refraining from unskillful actions, you are taking a step on the Buddha's path.

We each do so much, living overbooked, stressful lives; balancing work and nonwork life; balancing the needs of our family with our own; and so on. We become frustrated, overwhelmed, and rushed—and a manifestation of these perceived problems is seen in our actions. We have trouble with moderation when it comes to eating and drinking. We watch lots of television and Internet videos. We don't listen closely or pay attention, often doing things on autopilot. We are not in the present moment; instead we are mulling over the past or anticipating the future. We act with greed and appease our anger or suffering by consuming food and entertainment, among other things. We don't give to others or the community because we are so wrapped up in ourselves.

The wrongness of our actions is very evident when we do physical harm. But what if the wrongness is a more subtle matter: taking all the bread in the basket without regard for your dining companions, killing insects that get in your house, flirting with a neighbor, or drinking too much at a party? Did you hit the counter in a rage when your partner did not listen to your instructions? Did you speed to work because you overslept, endangering others on the road? These are actions that are clearly not "right" and do harm in some way, directly or indirectly. This book will discuss the positive and negative potentials our actions have.

The purpose of this book is to teach and remind us to be more aware, to make us all better and kinder in our dealings. This is a book of reminders for cultivating awareness in the area of Right Action. Just as with Right Speech, practicing Right Action is a very valuable tool in achieving happiness.

Greed drives us to work at jobs we do not like or that do not benefit others, all so that we can pursue our desires for a life filled with stuff. This book addresses that at length and hopes to relieve its readers of the "if only" way of thinking, for each fulfilled desire does not end the cycle of desire and attachment but perpetuates it. And generosity is not just about showing up or being there for one's family and friends, and it is not just about giving physical things like food and money. Generosity is about being there fully and with compassion—in both mind and body.

Being in the present moment is a big part of Right Action, too. If you wrote down everything you think about, you would see that a very large percentage of it is rehashing or remembering the past or planning, anticipating, or worrying about the future. Not being in the present moment means that we are not experiencing life to the fullest. We are adding in our judgments and likes and dislikes and opinions rather than seeing what is real and true.

This book is about trying to abandon wrong and harmful actions and at least striving to "do no harm." The book has three parts: a list of teachings that you can use to become more awake and aware during everyday life, including questions you can ask yourself and others; a series of short essays about topics pertaining to Right Action; and meditations focused on this part of the Noble Eightfold Path. The teachings, essays, and meditations point not just to what we do that is harmful, but also to the good we do and how to pay attention to and cultivate those actions. Moderation is discussed for all types of consumption, from eating and drinking to how we spend our leisure and entertainment time.

Spending a few minutes each day reading an essay or selecting a teaching to put on a sticky note to share with others will create a practice of mindfulness in which your actions match your highest values. Each time you choose the higher road in carrying out your actions, you will feel joy in bringing happiness to yourself and others.

Teachings

- Buddhist teachings refer to actions as being skillful (wholesome) or unskillful (unwholesome).

- Even if you have to rush, don't do a job just to get it done; that is a waste. Do it with all of your being.

- Recognize what you can do with your mind, and use this insight to make even the most mundane activities delightful and nourishing.

- Ask yourself if what you are about to do will be harmful. If your answer is yes, don't do it. Applying meditation before acting can ensure that nobody gets hurt.

- Practice mindful waiting. Use the opportunity to create a sacred moment. Breathe in and out three times, refreshing yourself through awareness.

- Awareness of an unwholesome action brings you closer to not repeating it in the future.

- You can cultivate the ability to perform Right Action by nondoing. Choosing to not act is like being the quiet center of a cyclone or hurricane.

- Plan to do something each day that gives you energy—something you love to do, something just for you.

- If you can look at situations with a balanced point of view, without attachment or indulging in harmful acts, you are living a proper life.

- When you are with kids, listen, care, be together, spend time, and respect what they say and do.

- Conscious attention to your actions and their consequences makes them a potent source of learning.

- Before you start the car, reflect for a moment on what you are doing and where you are going.

- Consider the idea of surrendering your actions to a higher power—not passively, but by being more alert to the intention and effect of everything you do.

- Gentle forbearance helps you restrain yourself long enough to determine the most skillful action for the moment.

- It means little if you love someone deep in your heart but the expression of this love is subverted or inhibited by anger, resentment, or alienation.

- No one controls who you are inside and what you choose to do—not really. And in the same way, you don't control who anyone else is and what anyone else does.

- From the moment you get up, and in everything you do throughout the day, be very mindful, making every act and thought meditation.

- You are heir to your own motives and deeds; your life does not unfold randomly or haphazardly.

- The way to achieve happiness is by engaging in positive actions and refraining from negative ones. Not only do you create your future happiness, but you make others happy, too.

- Act well in the moment and you will have performed a good action for all eternity.

- Each time you retaliate with aggressive words and actions, you are strengthening the habit of anger. As long as you do this, plenty of opportunities to be angry will come your way.

- Once you see how much better it is to do good than to do evil, you will begin to have even greater trust in your own inherent goodness.

- Voluntary simplicity is not just what you do but also the intention with which you do it.

- We often act out of habit. The more you can get in touch with your motivations, the more likely it is that you will act in ways that are in harmony with your deepest values.

- Get to know your own inner voice and don't be afraid to express it. Once you achieve this authenticity, everything you do will be fresh and special.

- Violence cannot be ended with violence; it can be ended only with compassion and understanding.

- When the mind wanders from what you are doing, bring it back. Repeat several billion times.

- You can inwardly thank someone who disturbs or harms you. Those who harm you are like teachers showing you the consequences of your actions.

- You can either change your actions or change your beliefs about those actions.

- When doing something skillful but intellectually undemanding, like painting a wall, take pride in carrying out the task to the best of your ability. Enjoy the process.

• In Zen, everything is in the doing—a doing arising from awareness—not in the contemplating. Everything one does becomes a potential vehicle for self-realization.

• For five minutes, do a silent running commentary on your actions: *I'm putting the key in the lock. I'm turning the key. I'm opening the door.* And so on. Later, see how much of those five minutes you can remember compared to any other period of your day.

• Recognize when you have choice—a choice to act or not. This allows more space in which to respond.

• Describing the character of your own thoughts as useful or not useful can help you avoid taking yourself too seriously.

- Make each move and action count. If you find yourself doing something twice, you were not mindful the first time.

- Meditation siphons off the pools of old collected experience, allowing you to skillfully and compassionately act in the present rather than react to the past.

- When you are angry, do not focus on the other person. Become the anger and allow it to happen within. Feel the wound and be grateful to the other person for helping you recognize what caused your anger.

- Generosity is the key to everything you really want. Act now.

- Be aware of the nondoer in the doing, the nonmover in the moving.

- Desire little, be content, and repay acts of kindness.

- You know that certain situations or circumstances produce unwholesome states within you, and you can act with determination not to pursue them.

- Take responsibility for past actions with an attitude of compassion, appreciating that an act may have been unwholesome or harmful and strongly determining not to repeat it.

- Imbue each act and each moment with mindful attention.

- Whenever you can find time for just being, drop all doing. "Thinking" is doing, "concentration" is doing, and "contemplation" is doing. For a moment, you are not doing anything and are just at your center.

- If you act with positive motivation, goodness is furthered.

- Skillful actions are rooted in compassion and wisdom and result in contentment. Skillful actions are the prerequisite to happiness, for us and others.

- When you start accepting your body, losing weight becomes less important and also easier. You create conditions for healing.

- Learning to go with the flow rather than resisting what you have to do can help you be more productive and enjoy your work more.

- Show compassion toward animals, and act on it: donate to an animal charity or try to eat more vegetarian meals.

- When you settle back and open yourself to what is happening in each moment without attachment or aversion, you are experiencing reality. From this attitude, you manifest true compassionate action.

- Be mindful of cause and effect. Notice how your actions, feelings, and thoughts influence others and your own state of mind.

- One compassionate word, action, or thought can reduce another person's suffering and bring him joy.

- Simply allow the mind to go free. Tell yourself you don't have to do anything. When there is no sense of having a task to do, the mind relaxes.

- When you turn on the television, it should be with awareness of what you are doing, even if all you want is a little escape to unwind from the pressures of the day.

- Show children that one does not create happiness through indulgence.

- When you realize that your attention has wandered off while doing a daily activity, notice the thought and return your attention to the activity. Notice the thought, return to the activity, notice the thought, return to the activity.

- Try to find time during the middle of the day for walking meditation, preferably outdoors.

- Start rearranging your priorities rather than taking life for granted. Learn to find joy in everything you do and in every interpersonal contact.

- Moments of stillness and genuine simplicity offer glimpses of what it means to live in a spiritual and free way.

- The more you practice the three trainings of ethics, meditation, and wisdom, the more difficult it will become for you to act in a way that is contrary to an ethical, compassionate attitude.

- Be honest with people about why you're unable to do what they ask, or why you've done something that doesn't suit them. This may involve giving more detail than you're used to.

- See how pain is reduced when, instead of resisting it, you do the opposite and open yourself to the pain.

- Actions that are kind, unselfish, and virtuous help others; help you accumulate good karma; and are an expression of wisdom, higher sanity, and enlightenment.

- You need wise reflection and consideration about where your actions are leading.

- Don't waste time dwelling on what might have happened if you'd taken a different path through life. Keep moving forward, choosing each new direction with care and a positive attitude.

- Diligence, patience, and generosity bring the conditions for happiness.

- You will suffer in this life and the next as a result of wrong actions. If you do good, you can achieve overwhelming happiness in this world, which will also be with you in the next.

- One must practice the things that produce happiness. When happiness is present, you have everything. If happiness is absent, you do everything in order to have it.

- Everything has implications—every thought, word, and deed has an effect, and absolutely everything you think, say, or do makes a difference.

- It means so much to a child to have a parent who really offers attention and listens. The parent and child are able to meet with openness and compassion.

- When you begin to feel overwhelmed, stop and look around. Looking literally at where you are can jolt your mind back to the present moment. Where am I? What is happening in this moment? What am I going to do about it?

- Paint, sing, dance, or do whatever you feel like doing to make this world a little more beautiful.

- Practice using a half smile to radiate well-being to yourself and coworkers. When you interact with others, do it in a warm, kind, and friendly way.

- Attachment to the self is the cause of all the harm, fear, and suffering in the world. Let go of the self and let go of fear and suffering—and stop doing harm.

- Take pride even in small responsible gestures, such as lowering your thermostat or recycling a glass bottle. Your action may end up saving future lives.

- Find a situation that is troubling you and which you have been trying to work out. Think about it and *do nothing*. Stop all unnecessary activity and thoughts regarding the situation. After about a week of this, note the changes that have taken place with the situation—without your having actively done anything about it.

- Act in a wholesome way and you will be happy.

- The secret to an awakened life is to be completely and deeply still, expansive, and present in the heart of whatever you are doing.

- What do you think is worthy of your attention? What will you give your precious time to? Attempt to be mindful of what you are doing and why.

- There are many places to volunteer to help others—senior organizations, hospitals, hospices, soup kitchens, literacy programs, schools, and local government.

- You cannot have a contented life if you unthinkingly say and do things that cause others (and yourself) suffering.

- Take the time to examine your motivations and to bring mindfulness to the feelings associated with the act you are about to perform.

- Consider how quickly you recover your balance if you trip. By the time you'd thought about how to arrest your fall, you'd be on the ground! Our bodies and their actions hold depths of wisdom.

- One compassionate word can give comfort and confidence, destroy doubt, help someone avoid a mistake, reconcile a conflict, and open the door to liberation.

- When you cultivate an awareness of the potential harm you cause through actions, you see that these actions harm you and also cause others and the environment to suffer.

- Learn to recognize when you've talked enough about your ideas and dreams and when it's time to put your planning into action.

- Improper sexual conduct springs from egotistical self-seeking, from selfish concern for your own desires. In any relationship, one must have concern for the other person.

- When you can see the world from the perspective that things are just as they are, your mind and heart will be at rest—no desire, no aversion, no envy, no jealousy.

- Be like bamboo and bend with the wind. If bamboo were stiff, it would break, but because it yields, it overcomes the wind.

- We all have the choice to be good or bad; no one makes the decision for us. Consider how a choice to do a bad thing hurts you and others.

- Meditation is not merely a matter of learning to focus your mind but also about bringing that state of concentration to even the smallest acts of your daily life.

- Impermanence is a principle of harmony. When you do not struggle against it, you are in harmony with reality.

- There is a difference between love and attachment. Love is an openness of heart, a spirit of generosity and interconnectedness. Attachment is driven by craving, desire, and greed.

- By developing the habit of mindfulness, you can make choices about how you will act or think.

- For your children, model the behavior of paying attention to the little things in life. Also, show them you do some good in your everyday life by being mindful, kind, and compassionate.

- Before a chess player makes a move, he must consider every option and multiple possible outcomes. He acts, his opponent responds, and new possibilities present themselves.

- Wise reflection and consideration help you see where your actions are leading.

- Practice awareness. Simply go for a walk. Simply listen to music. Simply eat a meal. Simply read. Keep your mind focused wholeheartedly on what you are doing.

- Start each day by reaffirming Right Intention. Remind yourself each day to work at letting go of ego, clinging, selfishness, controlling behavior, negative thoughts, possessiveness, aggression, resentment, and confusion.

- When you offer a gift or service, act wholeheartedly, in the true spirit of generosity, rather than merely going through the motions for appearance's sake.

- Mindfulness creates Right Action, which sensitizes you to your interrelations with other beings.

- Opportunities to help others lie latent in every moment. Stay alert for ways of doing good, of offering help, or of simply giving practical advice. Live generously in the community of souls.

- There is nothing special you have to do to eliminate unskillful states or to make skillful ones happen. All you have to do is be aware in the moment.

- Do not automatically turn on the radio or television, read while you exercise, or read while you are waiting. Just be.

- Love is being present, giving full attention, and really listening.

- As you go about your daily business, think of the energy you expend with every action. Good energy and intention beget good consequences and results.

- Practice mindful consumption and refrain from intoxicants and harmful substances that damage you, society, and the environment.

- A loving act ends up bearing loving fruit.

- Remember to connect to what you are doing. Each moment that you remember keeps you on the path to freedom.

- Use what might otherwise be considered dead time to focus your awareness on your immediate experience. Use your breath as the object of concentration.

- Things will go to pieces, but you do not have to fall apart when they do.

- The time you spend doing everyday tasks is precious. It is a time for being alive. When you practice mindful living, peace will bloom during your daily activities.

- When you live life with honesty and self-effacement, you are on the road to freedom.

- Open to the effortlessness of being rather than doing. Drop everything and let go.

- Seek to not be affected by what others say or do, no matter how cruel these acts may be.

- Say no when asked to do something you really do not want to do.

- Be a spiritual adventurer; be audacious. Take risks; search everywhere. Do not let a single opportunity that life offers pass you by.

- The desire for more, which is greed, is a root of unwholesome action.

- You can do without things; you are whole without these things. Refuse to be trapped by the trappings.

- Do unto others as you would have others do unto you.

- Acting in skillful ways leads to happy results.

- Gardening releases physical tension and reduces the amount of stress hormones circulating in the body, and the act of cultivation is in and of itself soothing for the soul.

- Think of a situation in which you acted badly or inappropriately. Note how your actions affected the other people involved. Breathe in the responsibility, pain, and other negative emotions. Breathe out forgiveness, understanding, and compassion.

- Love the people in your life. Love them by acting in harmonious ways, by bringing awareness to your behavior, and by acting with integrity.

- You do not want an identity that is a mask constructed to present an appealing image.

- If you feel unhealthy, take positive action. But if you feel strong and healthy, feel happy about it. Then turn your mind to concerns other than whether your body is perfect.

- No matter what you are doing, keep the undercurrent of happiness. Learn to be secretly happy within your heart in spite of all circumstances.

- You may be thinking, *It's time for another cup of coffee and one of those blueberry muffins.* It seems like it's always time to be doing something other than what you are doing at the moment.

- If you feel drowsy, mentally scan different points in the body. Feel the sensations at each place if they are accessible. Do this until you feel more alert.

- Look at things with more alertness. If you see a tree, stop for a while. Collect your awareness. When you are alert, you may perceive the tree differently.

- Things can be a certain way without needing to be acted upon or judged or even pushed aside. They can simply be observed.

- Things happen. That's all. You aren't really in control of the outcome. Your actions may influence things, but a lot of other factors influence things, too.

- The only real control you have is choosing your own thoughts, your own words, and your own actions.

- Doing your best is the only philosophy you will ever need, but you must follow through with action based on good intention.

- If you cannot accept and treat yourself with kindness, you cannot do the same for another person.

- One action can save a person's life or help someone take advantage of a rare opportunity.

- Ask yourself, Will this action take me in the direction that I want to go?

- Do things that contribute to your awareness, and refrain from those things that do not.

- Being grounded means having your attention completely inside your body no matter what you are doing.

- Remember that only an unhappy person acts in a nasty way.

- Finding beauty in the ordinary and the ordinary in beauty is spiritual life in action.

- The precept about abstaining from alcohol does not say you cannot have wine with dinner. It says to be aware of what happens when you drink too much and to avoid allowing that to happen.

- To create peace in the world, you must be unruffled within. Walk in stillness, and act in harmony. The serenity that emanates from you will create peace.

- The goal is not to rid oneself of or to transcend an emotion—not even hatred—but to regulate experience and action once an emotion is felt.

- In this life, we cannot necessarily do great things. But we can do all small things with great love.

- Restrain yourself from acting on angry impulses. Patience through mindfulness buys time. As soon as angry thoughts arise, you can apply the antidotes of patience and mindfulness.

- Practice mindful commuting. As you first sit, take three breaths. Be mindful and aware of the experience. Notice the environment. Be part of the journey. Be here now.

- Beginning is not only a kind of action but a frame of mind—a kind of work, an attitude, and a consciousness.

- The first step in growth is to do what you love to do and to become aware of doing it.

- Get up earlier. Doing so changes your life. Use the extra time for wakefulness and awareness. Use it as a time of stillness and presence.

- In your mind, see a lake with a smooth, glass-like surface. A breeze sends ripples across the water. As the breeze subsides, the water becomes smooth again. Remember this when something ruffles or disturbs you.

- Don't jump, lash out, or act out. If you are really dedicated to practicing patience, you can even learn to generate love and compassion on the spot when anger arises.

- Act as though it were impossible to fail.

- Refrain from saying or doing anything that might cause further damage or escalate anger.

- You can take responsibility for actions that are harmful, but you never deserve guilt, judgment, or shame. Understand that you have something to learn while loving yourself at the same time.

- Don't turn work into an escape from life, a substitute for love, or a way to make yourself more important than other people. Complete the work in full awareness of the present moment.

- Focus on the present moment and do your job.

- Drink a cup of tea. Do not think about drinking a cup of tea. Just drink it. Feel it. Enjoy it. Doing so is experience beyond thought.

- Sometimes with loved ones, you think you know them so well that you don't listen—don't hear what they are saying. You may also forget impermanence and expect them to not change.

- While driving, do a shoulder scan every once in a while: Notice where your shoulders are. Then, take a deep breath, and as you exhale lower your shoulders and feel the stretch in your neck.

- Identifying with your emotions and not understanding that pain and pleasure are impermanent leads to unskillful action.

- Too much analysis can lead to actions that are out of proportion to the problem you face. Always consider the simplest solution first. Avoid cutting a knot that you can untie.

- Take things one step at a time.

- Right Action means never doing anything that hurts others or yourself. Respect for others, reliability, kindness, and compassion are all key to this practice.

- Do the necessary things, the essential things, but pour more and more energy into watchfulness and awareness.

- Your actions are the result of past karma, and they also create new karma. To be aware of this reality and to master your actions are the keys to creating the karma of happiness.

- In the morning, spend five minutes writing without judging or worrying about its content. Simply cleanse your mind of any potential clutter.

- When sadness or anger rises up, do something completely different to break the pattern. If you feel angry at someone, go up and give them a big hug. Be innovative and imaginative.

- Decide that for one month, you will not take anything you are not sure you have permission to take—not even a glass of water. See what happens when you do this.

- Whatever the cause of your suffering, do not cause suffering for another.

- If you cultivate the habit of doing service deliberately, your desire for service will grow stronger and will make for not only your own happiness, but that of the world.

- Don't live like a robot. Everything you do is worth doing with total attention.

- Alcohol and drug abuse are harmful actions, but so are eating improperly and not getting enough sleep.

- If you want to eat everything in sight, stay with the experience and don't act on it. The feeling will take its course and dissipate.

- Begin to look not only at the expression of your actions but also at the repercussions of your actions. Realize that every mental and physical action has an effect.

- Choose a simple, regular activity that you usually do unconsciously or on autopilot. Do the activity with full attention instead. Try to bring mindfulness to that act each time. Add a new activity at the end of the week and build on your mindfulness and power of attention.

- The next time you're involved in a creative pursuit, try to initiate each breath and action from the fire in your belly. Its energy will feed your ideas and help you digest and deliver them.

- Wise avoidance is taking your attention out of the familiar groove of your habits. You need to see a habit as a habit—something you do not need to be bound to.

- Our quality of being is the ground of all appropriate action. When you look closely at your actions, you can see the quality of being behind your actions.

- One of the many rewards of acting with kindness is that it helps keep life simple.

- The better your mind gets at totally immersing itself in what you are doing, the less you will be plagued by distractions, desires, and fragmentation.

- Offering a calm and gentle smile is an act of peace. Looking with the eyes of compassion and making a peaceful step are gestures of peace and nonviolence.

• Pretend you are dying and there is nothing to be done. Rather than judging this news, take no position in your mind. Stop leaning into circumstances and instead rest in your own awareness.

• Restraint is the gentle discipline of settling back and allowing desires to arise and pass without always feeling the need or compulsion to act on them.

• Imagine that all your actions are like drops of water falling into a pond, and the ripples are signals you send out to those around you. This will help you see actions' consequences.

• Any gesture of kindness or honesty will affect how you experience your world. What you do for yourself you also do for others, and what you do for others, you do for yourself.

- Practice generosity and refrain from stealing.

- You may learn that the secret to living well is to "be" in the center of your "doing."

- Renounce one habit that you cling to. Replace it with open space. Try renouncing another poor habit or action each week.

- When meditating, forget the whole world and go in, turn in, and tune in, as if the world has disappeared and does not exist.

- What would happen if parents stopped worrying, obsessing, anticipating, and expecting? Being present with your family is an amazing feeling. Stop, and really pay attention to your kids.

- Make a point of bowing—in your mind or physically—to three people you are having difficulty with. Keep doing so until the difficulty is gone.

- Go to bed when you are moderately tired. Before that time, listen to gentle music, read a soothing book, or do a meditation. Rather than relying on an alarm, work toward awakening naturally when you need to awaken.

- If you can take a moment to settle yourself before the rush of the day begins, this act can serve as an anchor, a reminder that there is silence under the chaos.

- When you drink too much alcohol, the sense of knowing what is right and wrong falls away, and you lose the ability to abstain from doing harm.

- Even if you are only getting fast food at the drive-through window, be doing only what you are doing and pay attention to every detail.

- Wisdom replaces ignorance when you realize that happiness does not lie in the accumulation of more and more pleasant feelings.

- Not understanding the nature of likes and dislikes and clinging to them leads to unskillful action.

- Do a task with all of your being. Even if you have to rush, do not do a job just to get it done. That is a waste.

- Getting what you want does not always mean hard work and struggle. Often, it's when you relax and stop resisting that what you want can't resist you.

- When you are training your body at the gym, that should be the only thing you are doing.

- If you work with creative awareness, are present in your thoughts and actions, and fully inhabit each moment, you will find a flow and rightness in whatever you do.

- When you act unconsciously, you do and say things that hurt yourself and others. You react rather than respond, and it is reaction that creates most regrets in life.

- You might examine how you look at television. What do you watch? How much do you watch? How good is it? Is it a skillful or useful activity?

- You do not need to take irritations or annoyances personally or react to them.

- Focus your attention on sounds. They arise and pass away so you can experience the insight of impermanence. Be a satellite dish. This is a wake-up exercise for your attention.

- Free yourself from your mental conditioning through good works, through meditating, through laughter, through love, and through solitude.

- Transform feelings of guilt from negative action into creating a new positive action.

- Undertake each task with spirit, and eventually you will grasp the truth that every act is an expression of the Buddha nature.

- As you get ready to leave your home, consciously approach the door. Take three slow, deep breaths. Do you have what you need? Walk out the door and enter the world with your eyes wide open and a smile on your face.

- Peaceful sleep depends on knowing that you've acted well during the day.

- Do all activities with these intentions: to be gentle, kind, thoughtful, caring, compassionate, loving, fair, reasonable, and generous to everyone—including yourself.

- If you intentionally harm any being, whether through actions, thoughts, or words, you are more likely to harm again, probably with more insensitivity.

- When nothing is yearned for, you are free to enjoy what you do, free to see the patterns, and free to hear the music in all things.

- Do not be two-faced, acting pleasantly toward people in their presence only to show a different face when they are gone.

- Practice mindful breathing in any situation— while sitting, lying down, standing, driving, or working. Breathing consciously will bring more awareness and concentration to the action.

- Not causing any harm requires staying mentally awake. Part of being awake is slowing down enough to notice what you say and do.

- Kindness enables you to put your awareness into action by giving something of yourself. There are always opportunities in life for simple kindnesses.

- When you start to pay attention, your relationship to things changes. You see more and see deeply. Knowing what you are doing while you are doing it is the essence of mindfulness.

- When you understand what your motivation is, you may choose to act differently.

- Try doing manual labor in a sacred manner, just doing what you are doing as if it is the ultimate divine service.

- If you want to know what you were doing in the past, then look at your body and present situation, because it was shaped by past actions. If you want to know what your situation will be in the future, look at what you're doing with your mind now.

- Good motivation for every action is essential. For example, do not eat merely to satisfy your hunger. Eat to maintain strength, prolong your life, and serve others.

- Many of us try to do more and more. We do things because we think we need to. We do things without thinking because we are in the habit of doing them. With an attitude of accomplishing, judging, or grasping, there is not Right Action.

- The phrase "take your time" is an important one; it is your time, and it's up to you what you do with it. Don't fill silences with words and action; relax and give yourself time to ponder.

- Refrain from mindless consumption and forgo using products and services that unduly harm animals, plants, humans, and nonsentient life.

- During summer, commit to one hour during which you will not kill any bug. Become aware of your emotions, frustrations, and desire to kill. What happens when you do not kill?

- Try the thirty-day list: Write down what you want. Then, thirty days later, see if you still want or need what's on the list.

- While in the car, say kind things to other drivers: "May you safely reach your destination. May you find the happiness and fulfillment that you are seeking."

- Act positively for the benefit of others—in the workplace, in the family, everywhere you go. Consciously practice nonharming by not engaging in any act that causes harm to yourself or others. And be an example to others.

- You may feel much more in control when you bring awareness to what you are doing while you are doing it.

- Each one of us experiences wrong understanding, from time to time, of what we see and remember. This gives rise to delusion, greed, and hatred. Wrong understanding leads to unskillful action.

- The next time you are about to lose it, be aware of the accompanying body sensations. These indicate that what you are about to say or do may be harmful.

- Beware of performing tasks on autopilot. Unless you fully engage, your mind wanders and your efficiency and productivity suffer.

- You are the victim of your own suffering, and because you do not know how to handle it, you hurt others when you are in pain. Become responsible for your own pain.

- Try to be mindful of your movements. Take a few mindful breaths to relax your body and mind. Do your best to make your steps and actions peaceful ones.

- Each time you are provoked, you are given a chance to do something different. You can strengthen old habits of anger, or you can weaken them by seeing the anger and letting it go.

- We live immersed in a world of constant doing. Remind yourself to be mindful. Moments of mindfulness are moments of peace and stillness, even in the midst of activity.

- Do a major time-management audit every few months. Consider which routine activities are intruding into your quality of life and whether you could shed any of them.

- How much do you give back?

- Whatever you are doing, take the attitude of wanting it to directly or indirectly benefit others.

- Whenever you act motivated by greed, hatred, or delusion, pain and suffering come back to you.

- Do the things you have to do, and if you have time do some things you want to do.

- Action may not always bring happiness, but there is no happiness without action.

- You will suffer if you expect other people to conform to your expectations, if you want others to like you, if you do not get something you want, and so on.

- Part of being awake is slowing down enough to notice what you say and do. Make it your way of life to stay awake, slow down, and notice.

- Realize that being who you want to be and doing what you want to do lead to self-respect.

- When you are feeling down or otherwise not quite right, try making mindful, slow movements, like those in tai chi.

- Friends should be charitable, hospitable, and loyal. Friends should speak and act pleasantly and work for each other's welfare. Friends should treat each other as equals.

- Happiness comes not from having much but from being attached to little.

- Ask yourself, What do I really want? Would I know it if I got it? Does everything have to be perfect or under my total control for me to be happy right now? Is everything basically okay right now? Are there decisions or steps I can take that would move me toward peace and harmony?

- You do all those things for which you criticize all those people in your life whom you don't like—all those people you judge.

- When an opportunity comes, do not let it pass by, yet always think twice before acting.

- Experience simple, repetitive work such as sewing, washing your face, or brushing your teeth as meditation in action, focusing totally on the moment at hand and nothing else.

- How much of what you do is important and truly necessary?

- The practice of mindful living helps you stop to see what you are doing and where you are heading.

- Whatever you have started to do, accomplish that very thing first. Do everything well in this way, otherwise nothing will be achieved.

- If you plant wheat, wheat will grow. If you act in a wholesome way, you will be happy. If you act in an unwholesome way, you water the seeds of craving, anger, and violence in yourself.

- When done mindfully, the act of scrubbing the sink takes on the same beauty as watching the sunset.

- Try to be balanced in everything you do, including eating.

- Stop what you're doing and think about the sensations in your body, being part of humanity, and your relationships. You've momentarily relieved yourself of the burden of habitual thinking.

- If you practice mindful walking and deep listening all day long, you are practicing meditation in action.

- The antidote to hatred is tolerance. Tolerance enables you to refrain from acting angrily because of the harm inflicted on you by others. Tolerance protects you from being conquered by hatred.

- Whatever you do and however you act creates how you become, how you will be, and how the world around you will be.

- Happiness comes from acting with the knowledge that you don't have much time, so you live with fullness, attention, and impeccability.

- Act with kindness to act with kindness, not to fulfill your duty or earn brownie points.

- Whatever you are doing, keep attentive to the gap between the in-breath and the out-breath. Focus on that gap; do not stop your activity. This attentiveness reveals two layers of existence: doing and being.

- How you act and think creates new habits and conditions for how you will act and think in the future.

- Think only and entirely of what you are doing at the moment, and you are free.

- Dive in without paying attention to resistance, and you'll get it done. Go with the flow and do your job.

- As a general rule, caring for others is the best thing you can do.

- If you delegate a task to a colleague, recognize that he or she may carry it out differently than you would have. Give the person the freedom to act.

- People who do hurtful deeds will damage themselves by their actions.

- Be so busy that you don't have time to look for happiness; have work to do and be content with the work.

- It's often been said that we become the choices we make. Our identity is developed through the way we behave and act—especially toward other people.

- Hand washing is both a practical and symbolic act of preparation.

- The Buddha stressed that the practice of the precepts of Right Action is the basis of Right Concentration, Right Mindfulness, and Right Understanding.

- For one week, act on every single thought of generosity that arises spontaneously in your heart.

- Attend to the taste of your food when chewing and swallowing, even sensing the food going into the digestive system.

- Close your eyes and consider how your actions impact your own life and the lives of those around you. Resolve that you will make an effort to respond to all situations with generosity, kindness, and thoughtfulness.

- Delusion can be a potent and damaging force in your life. By harmonizing your actions with the way life really is, you can disable this force and keep yourself free.

- Without holding or pushing away, without accepting or rejecting, you can move along with daily work, doing what needs to be done and helping wherever you can.

- When you are angry, you can choose to calm down so that your actions will not flow from anger.

- Watch television mindfully, not mindlessly. When you turn off the television, it should be with awareness of what you are doing and why.

- Be patient with yourself and do not lose your sense of perspective.

- Each person in the chain of karma has a choice about how to act. Each can choose to not act on a seed of anger. Each person can take action with strength, compassion, and love.

- Abstain from any kind of dishonesty or any kind of misappropriation or exploitation, because these are expressions of craving and desire.

- Take a moment to appreciate how you have been mindful in your work or school or other tasks each day. Consider how you can build on that the next day.

- Remember that whatever you do has a result; what goes around comes around.

- As you become more in touch with a sense of yourself as beautiful, you will feel less compulsion to seek things outside of yourself through unethical actions.

- You can repeatedly return from mindless moments in your daily life to awareness of what you are doing.

- If you practice mindful living, anger will not overwhelm you.

- Learn to quiet your mind at will. When you look inward and watch your own mental habits in action, do not judge them. Be still, as an observer or witness. In stillness, you will discover the truth.

- Act in a way that will give no one a reason to criticize.

- Let everything become an opportunity to watch. The more watchful you become, the more you slow down and become graceful. Your chattering mind becomes quiet and clear.

- Watch your words; they become your actions. Watch your actions; they become your habits.

- Bring to mind something you have done or said that you feel was a kind or good action. Enjoy the happiness that comes with this memory. Meditate on good and kind action.

- *Namaste* means "The divine in me salutes the divine in you." You can greet anyone in this way, acknowledging our interconnectedness.

- Whenever you cross a threshold, go through a doorway, or enter a room, see it as entering a temple, and do so reverently.

- When you lose your focus and the ability to consciously choose what to do, mentally stop. Smile to yourself. Chide yourself gently. Then breathe.

- Kids benefit from responsibilities, which help their self-esteem.

- When you have completed an action, stop and feel the energies of that moment.

- Living in the moment does not mean acting impulsively, without thought of the future.

- When you have a project to do, set a timer for thirty minutes and focus only on that activity. When you get distracted, note the distraction and refocus on the task at hand.

- Even if all you can do is greet your mental storm with acceptance, doing so creates more peace.

- The more meditation you do, the more you naturally get in touch with yourself. You will become more aware of what you are doing on a moment-by-moment basis.

- Treat others with the mind of giving, and practice doing deeds that have no reward.

- Contentment comes from neither doing nor having but being.

- Rejoice in whatever life gives you. Do not crave otherwise. Know that whatever you have been given is for your own good.

- Do the one thing that really makes you happy when you are very sad.

- Sit, stop, and become a human still life. Do nothing, be nothing—except breathe.

- Negative emotions need your permission before they enter into your heart. No one can force you to be unhappy; you always have the right of refusal.

- Practice the gentle letting go of distracting thoughts. Do not judge yourself or try to figure out why or what you were thinking. This is the powerful practice of beginning again.

- Relationships are about living with each other in ways that are kind, in which you hear each other and refrain from hurting through anger or violence.

- Go on a media fast for a few days: no television, movies, radio, music, Internet, or reading. Try just sitting by yourself, doing nothing. Notice what you feel. These are the feelings you normally avoid by keeping yourself occupied.

- Choose any action in your day that you take for granted. Bring to that activity the clear intention to attend closely to all its details.

- Adults often discuss how kids give in to peer pressure, but adults need to see that they do exactly the same thing.

- Recognize that conflicts are inevitable, and resolve to meet them with love and kindness.

- If you let go of your preconceptions about yourself, your life, and your work, you may find that your mind expands. That room is helpful for concentrating on and immersing yourself in your work.

- When you intend to act, move, or speak, first examine your mind and then proceed appropriately and with composure.

- When your logical mind becomes an obstacle to effective decision making, block out its chatter and noise and tune in to your heart. Listen carefully, and you will find mental balance.

- If you make a vow, stick to it. If it is worth doing, do it properly.

- Take time for yourself for sitting meditation. Do not feel guilty about taking this time.

- Relaxation is a natural response that you allow to happen. It is what is left when you stop creating tension. Relaxation is not something that you *do*.

- Before you act, stop for a moment and think: *Am I about to be helpful or harmful? Skillful or unskillful? Selfless or selfish?*

How Would Buddha Act?

- Choose a routine activity you perform several times each day. Resolve to do that activity mindfully for a week, noting your intention before each component of the activity.

- When an unskillful action is performed, its seed is implanted in the mind. When the right circumstance comes, this dormant seed will germinate as another unskillful action that causes suffering.

- When washing the dishes, treat each dish and utensil as if it is sacred. Follow your breath. Do not hurry. Consider this task to be the most important thing in life.

- If you do something, be very observant, careful, and alert. Put the dough in the oven and watch it transform.

- Spend at least five minutes of each meal in silence. If you do have a conversation, keep the topics light and supportive.

- Practice making friends with yourself, accepting yourself fully. Soften and open your heart to yourself first, which will ultimately lead you to do the same for others.

- Recognize and identify when you create bad karma: *When I think like this, speak like that, listen like this, or act like that, my suffering increases.*

- Analyze how mindfulness affects a routine task and how you see the world. Try to recall the details of the task after you have performed it mindfully. This gives you an understanding of how often you could be paying closer attention and how that attention can change the routineness into something that feels fresh.

- Slow down. When you review those actions that have caused you remorse, you will often find that they were undertaken in haste.

- Really do what you are doing. Be awake and alive as you do it, remaining mindful of the tendency to go on autopilot.

- Focus on what you are doing; be mindful. Doing so frees you from thoughts of winning or losing; you will be unattached to the outcome.

- You never do anything well till you cease to think about the manner in which you do it.

- All activities should be done with one intention: to help, not harm, others.

- Mindful living is an art. You can practice it anytime, even while driving or doing work.

- Let action flow naturally from your resolve. If there is a waiting period before you can actually embark on what you've chosen to do, use it to affirm your trust in yourself.

- Recognize that you are not separate from all that exists, and commit to a culture of nonviolence and reverence for life.

- When you catch yourself being habitual, spontaneously do something different. Every time you do this, it will become harder to slip into habit unconsciously.

- Stop, sit down, and become aware of your breathing once in a while throughout the day. Fully accept the present moment and how you are feeling. Do not wish for anything to change; just breathe and let go.

- Imagine you are running through a dark forest. You reach a clearing and rest there momentarily. Pause and take deep breaths. Then you see a path leading out of the forest. You follow it and emerge back into sunlight.

- Every action ripples through the community of souls. Make an effort to ensure that your ripples have positive effects when they make landfall.

- As an experiment, think of everything as a dream created by your consciousness. Maintain this awareness as you live and act.

- Learn what you can from your experiences; act on that learning; and then share with others, by example, what you have learned.

- Once you are fully aware, you will understand what is the Right Action to take.

- Whenever you engage in a selfless action that contributes to the welfare of others, you create a vibratory pattern that will lead you into higher states of mind.

- You can cultivate a way of living that brings you increasingly into connection with goodness.

- Disregard whatever you think yourself to be, and act as if you are absolutely perfect—whatever your idea of perfection may be. Behave as best you know, and do what you think you should.

- A single act of laziness, selfishness, or mean-spiritedness can lead to a long detour from the Noble Eightfold Path.

- Examine your mental states while you go about your actions. As soon as a delusion develops that would cause you to act inappropriately, try to firmly face the delusion and let it go.

- If your schedule is busy, prioritize your activities and do the most important ones first.

- Bring grace to all your endeavors. Before you do something, stop and feel the energy of the moment. Become completely present while doing the action.

- It does not matter whether somebody did something for you or not; you can still offer this person your love and compassion. Look this person in the eyes and don't hold back.

- It's never too late to do nothing.

- When you realize that happiness comes not from pushing away but from letting go, not from grasping but from opening to the moment, you can cultivate compassion within yourself.

- The more you are concerned about the happiness of others, the more you are building your own happiness. Do not expect anything in return. Think only of what is good for the other person.

- With a compassionate state of mind, your actions will always carry a tone of kindness and softness, which is very useful in overcoming difficulty with others.

- Go to the quietest place you know. Sit and let your mind and body settle. Let everything in this setting fade until you are left with an experience of emptiness.

- Analyze your life closely. If you do, you will eventually find it difficult to misinterpret the seeking of money or stuff as the path to happiness.

- If you have people who are difficult to deal with, be neither attracted nor repulsed. Be the bigger person.

- When you are mindful, you know you are doing something as you do it rather than performing on autopilot.

- Practice acting on the thoughts of generosity that arise in your mind.

- Rebirth every morning gives you the feeling of urgency, which is an important ingredient of spiritual life.

- Even the smallest action done with loving appreciation of life can touch other human beings in a profound way.

- One does not need to believe in the law of gravity to drop a coin into a needy person's hand: all this action needs is love, and the coin falls.

- If a person speaks or acts with a pure thought, happiness follows this person like a shadow that never leaves.

- Aim to live in a state of simplicity and nonaction—simply being rather than constantly doing and achieving.

- If you want release from suffering, then be done with doubt and let go of rampant desires.

- Drop the imaginary person in your head who goes on and on talking, asking questions, judging, and calculating everything. You do not need this person.

- In every situation, resting in openness and acting with kindness is the right answer.

- No harm will come to you if you undertake no harmful actions.

- Try varying the times of day when you do repetitive jobs, or look for ways to do things entirely differently. Elements of change and experimentation can enliven the most tiresome chore.

- Do you have the patience to wait until the mind settles and the water is clear? Can you be quiet for a moment, until the right words or actions arise?

- Freedom from thought does not mean no thought. It means that thoughts come and go freely. You don't latch onto them.

- Have lunch with people you like, or have a quiet lunch alone. You can also take a walk or do some type of exercise during your lunch break.

- Let a bell or some other sound remind you to put thought into your actions. When you respond to the sound, do so with awareness.

- Look at the person you're angry with and try to remember something nice that person said or did.

- If an act is motivated by true kindness, it will bring a positive result.

- Write "What am I doing?" on a piece of paper and hang it where you will see it often. This note will help release you from thinking about the past or the future and return you to the present moment.

- There's no need to put on an act to be noticed in social gatherings; just open your heart and mind and let grace flow gently into the room.

- Act as if it is your duty to be happy.

- You can nourish mindfulness by doing anything you truly enjoy, such as cooking or gardening.

- To be courageous is to take a flying jump. Commitment plus courage takes you right where you want to be.

- Take a breath; take a break. Cultivate the power of the present moment. Lie down, sit, stand—it does not matter. Let everything else subside.

- Acting with virtue takes you toward the wind of enlightenment. Acting from virtue leads to virtue, which leads to happiness.

- You can understand karma directly as the development of habits; each habitual action strengthens a tendency to repeat the action.

- Every act of generosity weakens the factor of greed.

- As if you were training a puppy, gently bring your mind back from distraction with mindful breathing. You can gradually learn to calm and center yourself using the breath.

- What if you strove to be generous, kind, and thoughtful all the time, releasing any thoughts of self-gain as a result of these good actions? Good karma depends on pure intentions.

- Without self-blame, return your attention to what is in front of your nose. When you do this as gently as possible, it becomes natural and spontaneous.

- Work at allowing more things to unfold in your life without forcing them to happen and without rejecting the ones that do not fit your idea of what should be happening.

- Cultivate your own spirit. Do not go looking for something outside of yourself.

- Ask yourself, How do I want to live this day?

- Battling against darkness is of little use to the seeker. Taking up arms against the negative brings the negative into your heart. What you must do instead is let in the light.

- Do a standing meditation while waiting in line for a movie or bus or train. Just stand there, breathe, and awaken.

- Just do what you are doing without thinking about it. Just be where you are without holding on or running away. Give up judging and spectating and dive into this moment.

- Note how your mind adds to stress. Gently set the fabrications of your mind aside. Return to paying mindful attention to whatever you are doing.

- Practice receiving violent words and actions aimed at you and transforming them into flowers, like the Buddha. The power of understanding and compassion give you the ability to do this.

- Practice contentment and refrain from sexual misconduct.

- Make two little piles of pebbles each day: one for positive actions and one for negative actions. Count the positives and negatives when considering an action.

- The peace, kindness, and humility with which you do a job are ways to bring spirituality into the workplace.

- Bad actions committed by a person will eventually return to cause suffering for that person.

- The ear is a door; it allows sound to enter your life. Listening can also allow a great silence to come into your life. When you listen, a great peace starts falling on and showering you.

- When you see others being treated unfairly, take carefully considered action. Stand up to the bully or expose injustice. Your values keep you from being a passive bystander.

- Realize that complete satisfaction does not exist, and instead, set your sights on being generally satisfied and generally happy.

- You do not need perfect quiet to meditate. It isn't noise that bothers you; it is your judgment about the noise.

- If you are able to maintain continuous mindfulness, nothing will upset you. You will not become angry or agitated. You can be patient no matter what anyone says or does.

- Practice love, and refrain from killing anything physically or mentally.

- Small acts of selflessness make for a compassionate life. Share anything you're given, if at all possible, and let others decide how you'll jointly spend your leisure time.

- Choose to not feel injured by others' speech and actions; instead, have compassion. Your compassion transforms their actions.

- People consume unmindfully because they do not know how to handle their suffering. You can make and maintain lasting, healthy change when you feel the joy of living.

- If you have a decision to make, stop for a moment and close your eyes. Focus on your breath. Listen with your heart for intuitive guidance on what to do next.

- The choice you exercise must make you comfortable and at peace. Choices that are made out of fear and anxiety often do not lead to Right Action.

- When you give to others, your unselfishness removes the spot of "self" that has stained your awareness.

- Nail biting is something you do just to deal with energy that is there and is too much to bear. If you live more energetically and intensely, then you will find that a habit such as nail biting disappears on its own.

- When you enter a room, be in a continuous flow, mindful of what you are doing.

- When thoughts or melodies go through your head, be glad for them. Then bring your attention back to what you were doing.

- Suffering is the process of trying to get and hold on to that which we like while trying to avoid and eliminate that which we do not like.

- When you sense that someone is seeking your approval, commend this person if you can do so without betraying your values. To give the reassurance this person needs will cost you nothing.

- Watch the breath like a visitor. Know what it is doing—keep following it—while simultaneously awakening the mind. Eventually all that remains will be the feeling of wakefulness.

- When you rest your utensil between bites and don't put more food in your mouth before you finish chewing and swallowing what's already there, you will raise your awareness of eating.

- Since you don't have any control, all you can do is go along for the ride—maybe even relax and enjoy it.

- Do you remember people's names after you've been introduced to them? Can you summarize the plot of the movie you just saw? If the answer is no, you may want to work on paying attention.

- If the quality of your being is poor—if you feel angry or worried—then your actions will be poor.

- Right Action is reverence for all life and respect for the property of others. It is the practice of love and nonviolence.

- If you don't build your world on expectations, it will not collapse when things turn out differently.

- Take care of the thoughts, and the actions will take care of themselves.

- The purpose of your life is not just to solve your own problems and find happiness but to free every living being from all of its suffering.

- Try to meditate for one minute of every hour throughout the day. Stop whatever you are doing and follow the breath with full attention for sixty seconds.

- If you are feeling anxiety, first notice how anxiety is nothing more than spinning your wheels. Then say, "I am sick of thinking about this. Instead of feeling anxious, here are three things I can do."

- Take a moment—midactivity—to find your center, regroup, and remind yourself of what is important, who you are, where you are, what you are doing, what you can and can't control, and what is really happening now.

- The more you are mindful of your thoughts, speech, and actions, the more insight you will have into the nature of your own suffering and the suffering of others. You will then know what to do and what not to do in order to live joyfully and in peace.

- The more complicated the world gets and the more intrusive it becomes in your psychological space and privacy, the more important it will be to practice nondoing.

- Why be unhappy about something if you can do something about it? If nothing can be done, how does being unhappy help?

- Adapt yourself to circumstances, just as water adapts to a vessel.

- Use a neighbor's barking dog for a meditation focus. Focus on the sound without judging. Do this to let the dog barking become your teacher instead of your tormentor.

- You help alleviate your own suffering when you help alleviate the suffering of others. Go and do something good for someone else.

- Have the courage to open your heart, face reality, admit mistakes, and take Right Action.

- Do something peaceful, magical, and serene in the evening. Go for a walk before dinner, light candles or incense, take a long bath, or prepare dinner in a ritualized manner. Or just sit and meditate. Take the time to release the day's cares, tensions, and stresses.

- Go outside on a peaceful night and scan the sky for one star. Focus on the star. Think about what it is. Listen to the messages of the star and the universe.

- Pay close attention to exactly what you are eating and how it affects you. Start eating more slowly. Be more aware of your impulses to use food to satisfy psychological needs.

- Read and do mini breathing meditations— even if only for five seconds—at the end of each paragraph. Pause and take a conscious breath. Then move on.

- Avoid all bad things; only do good things and cleanse your actions.

- Act on an intuitive feeling.

- Try this focus in meditation: I act, but I am not my actions. I think, but I am not my thoughts.

- Discipline moves you beyond the ignorance of thinking you can do whatever you want.

- Observe the relationship between thoughts and actions.

- Do you assume that you know what your loved ones want to do, what they want to eat, or where they want to go? It is important to really listen to what your loved ones say and allow for the changes they undergo.

- Learn first aid. Knowing what to do to help others if a crisis occurs is a wonderful gift.

- If your actions, speech, and thoughts are determined by greed, ill will, and delusion, then you will continue to intensify the suffering in your life.

- Feeling good is worth far more than looking good, and it makes you attractive. Resist the temptation to check your appearance in a mirror. The real you is the one looking out.

- See and take the best opportunities that present themselves to you. Say no to any invitation or request that goes against the values and goals you've set for yourself.

- Some long for change; others fear change. Be in a third group: those who strive to change what they can and should change.

- Can you think of something else to do at this moment that will be healthier and more personally satisfying than eating?

- Be aware of actions, emotional states, intentions, and mental and physical reactions. Make an effort to be fully aware. Let emotional states, opinions, and passing thoughts go.

- Actions that lead not to distress, but to a bright and cheerful heart, are good karma.

- When you have Right Understanding of impermanence and karma, you are motivated to practice the precept of nonharming with your children, which means you will not engage in any act that harms them.

- Reflect on the supposed importance of a modern convenience, such as a dishwasher. Reflect on and appreciate the people and hard work involved in creating this object. Thank all of them.

- When driving, be observant. Everything is constantly changing, and each situation requires different responses. Being observant is actually meditation while moving.

- You do not need to indulge the mind's every desire and impulse; learn to say no to the mind, gently and with humor.

- Energy levels change in the mind as well as the body. In a low energy state, keep your eyes open and try noting the beginning and ending of each breath.

- Meditation is nondoing. Meditation does not involve trying to get somewhere else. It emphasizes being where you already are.

- When you embrace the Five Precepts of Buddhism, you change your karma, your actions, and the fruits of your actions.

- Your actions should demonstrate generosity, patience, awareness, wisdom, and discipline.

- To focus more closely on any activity, choose one sense (hearing, seeing, tasting, touching, or smelling) and see how much more information you can take in than you usually do.

- Once you have your own self in order, then you can help others do the same.

- When you try to control others, you are focusing on somebody else instead of being mindful of your own actions.

- Happiness cannot come from without. It is not what you see and touch or what others do for you that makes you happy; it is that which you think and feel and do.

- Chaos is inherent in all complex things. Strive on with diligence in the face of chaos.

- Try adding contemplation to your actions. When you are sweeping, you can be removing anger or fear. When you are mowing, you can be cutting down desire and greed.

- There may be things you would like to do or say, but you don't do them or say them because they are dishonest or hurtful.

- Learn how to work with all your reactions so that you may be less controlled by them—so that you may see more clearly what you should do and how you might respond effectively.

- Happiness comes from letting go.

- Practice consciously doing one thing at a time. Do whatever you're doing more slowly, more intentionally, and with more awareness and respect.

- Whatever you do, do it wholeheartedly and with full awareness—even breathing.

- Before you get out of bed each morning, take five minutes to lie very still. Listen, see, smell, and breathe. Do not judge; just observe.

- Allow your actions to flow from the innocence of your heart.

- For whatever words you have said or actions you have committed that have caused harm, ask forgiveness. Forgive the words and actions others have expressed that have harmed you. Be at peace.

- If you can learn the lessons that challenging experiences are giving you, you do not have to go through the same lessons over and over again.

- You do not have to lose your temper if you see the action's intention before acting upon it. You can let the anger go, dropping it so it never comes to fruition.

- As much as possible, engage in virtuous activity with a good attitude. Develop a rough understanding of the nature of reality or maintain a wish to do so and work at it.

- Appreciate the time you have. Do not feel driven to fill it up without stopping to reflect on your life.

- Stop, notice, and appreciate what is happening. Even if this is all you do, it is revolutionary.

- When you are impatiently wanting the toaster to work faster, wake up! Breathe, smile, and settle into the present moment. Cultivate a patience practice out of this type of experience.

- A project or chore that you don't want to do is exactly what you make it: something interesting or a pain; your pick.

- Meditation helps enlarge your perspective beyond identifying with self-obsessed thoughts and opinions. You have more patience and tolerance than you know.

- You may often confuse your true self with external things, such as your body or possessions. Awareness separates these perceptions and helps you move toward clear thinking.

- You need to understand the consequences of harmful actions and restlessness, especially compulsive planning.

- It doesn't matter what anyone else thinks or does, because you can't control what anyone else thinks or does.

- Take a few moments to reflect on the emotions that hold the greatest power in your life or where you most easily become lost. Experience the freedom within your heart from simply letting go.

- Pick one activity that you do every day and practice doing it mindfully.

- Let things be as they are, and accept all that you like and dislike with equanimity. Be at peace, neither pulling anything to you nor pushing anything away.

- Sing at your work! You will do more in the same time, you will do it better, and you will persevere longer.

- When you understand that unfair, harmful, or hateful actions rebound in suffering, you can respond to them with compassion rather than anger or resentment.

- Some people take refuge in television to evade the real issues in their lives. They cannot turn it off because they would have to return to themselves, which is uncomfortable.

- An unwholesome or negative state of mind cannot arise at the same moment as a moment of mindfulness.

- Spouses and partners should be compassionate, committed, devoted, faithful, loyal, respectful, and understanding.

- Work to transform what you do rather than what you think. This will lead to changes in the way you see the world, and before you know it, your thoughts will calm down.

- When you eat and read the newspaper, just eat and read the newspaper. Be aware of the doing and be thankful.

- Extraordinary benefits come from the simple act of paying attention.

- Before a meal, you can join your palms in mindfulness and think about the people who do not have enough to eat.

- Bring awareness to how you end your meditation. Do not judge how it ends, but look at it closely. See the transition simply for what it is.

- Refrain from actions that create more fear and confusion.

- Peace is in the doing; it is not being inside a quiet room. Move the anxiety you attach to an activity out of the way. You can have stillness and keep moving, too.

- When you know that doing something leads to harm for yourself and others and is not done by people who are wise, do not do it.

- Taking air, energy, or water that you do not need is stealing; you are taking these resources away from someone else and creating suffering.

- Not understanding the natural aging and decay of the body leads to unskillful action.

- When you are criticized, you naturally want to justify yourself. If you use good principles of thought and conduct, you can rest easy, even when people disagree with what you did.

- Performing acts of kindness significantly increases happiness. Try to do at least five kind acts a week, no matter how big or small.

- When your actions are motivated by generosity, love, or wisdom, the results are happiness and peace.

- Recall those times when you looked into your partner's eyes and saw the pain you caused. Remind yourself that you caused this person you love to suffer. If you can see how hurtful your actions were and have concern for your partner's well-being, then compassion and loving-kindness will come, and you will act better in the future.

- Love is the ultimate way to transform people, even when they are full of anger and hatred. You need tremendous patience to do this continually and steadily.

- Do a thank-you prayer for the gift of sight, the gift of hearing, the gift of smell, the gift of taste, and the gift of touch.

- When you decide to solve your problems by getting angry or greedy, you become trapped by those actions. You suffer much more.

- Compassion is the source of nonviolent action, and it brings you inner strength and mental peace. These qualities bring more smiles, friendship, and harmony.

- Mindfulness is the practice of stopping and becoming aware of what you are thinking and doing.

- Your morning sets the trend for the whole day. Laughter is the best thing to start it with. Then, throughout the day, whenever there is the least opportunity, laugh!

- Morality is a big part of Right Action. Morality comes from Right Understanding, insight, good intentions, and good feelings.

- The more you maintain focus, the more it carries over into everything you do, no matter how large or small the task.

- Meditation can be done anywhere, such as at your desk for a few minutes.

- Every human action may be undertaken as an exercise toward enlightenment.

- Lighten up and find joy in whatever needs to be done.

- When you love someone, you don't try to change that person. Love accepts someone as he or she is; attachment wants that person to do things your way.

- Taming your mind is not a hobby or an extracurricular activity; it is the most important thing you could be doing.

- Happiness lies in a constructive job done well. Get happiness from your work, or you may never know what happiness is.

- Find a situation in your life that is limiting. Walk right through it today. Do not think about how. Just do it. Do this every day for a week.

- You cannot change the past, arrange the future to suit you, or make other people say and do the things you want them to say and do.

- Just as you must examine your life and determine how to best practice nonharming—not engaging in any act that causes harm to yourself or others—you can also practice doing good.

- Stop all the doing by shifting into "being mode" for a moment. Think of yourself as an eternal witness, as timeless. Just watch this moment without trying to change it at all.

- Only when you are mindful can you seize opportunities for conscious choices, act with kindness, and avoid hurting others through your actions and words.

- The motivation behind the act makes it violent or nonviolent.

- When you promise yourself to never repeat a mistake, convert the promise into an affirmation that you say out loud to yourself, or write it in a notebook that you refer to regularly.

- Increase your awareness of the intentions that drive your actions. Sit with each intention before deciding to follow it. Consider the decision to follow or not follow as a separate moment unto itself. The more aware you are of the nature of your intentions, the more choice you have in whether or not you act on them.

- Pay closer attention to your actions and to signs from the universe that you may be making errors in judgment.

- Attend to the contemplation of every detail in the action of eating: looking at and seeing the food, bringing the food to the mouth, the food touching the mouth, placing the food in the mouth, the mouth closing, taking the hand away, and chewing.

- Your actions have consequences for others and the world, even if you are not aware of what the consequences are. The way to become aware is through pure seeing.

- Remember that if you do not live in goodness, you are not happy. To live with a sincere heart is to live in peace. This is not a wish, but a fact.

- Kindness and compassion do not always mean saying yes.

- Children can help you enter into beginner's mind—that state before concepts, conditioning, and defenses insulate you from experiencing directly. Allow their joyfulness to inspire you.

- Since we are all connected in this ocean of life, everything we do comes back to us.

- As your mindfulness grows sharper, you will begin to be aware of your actions before taking them.

- Whatever situation you are in, you can stop long enough to allow yourself to be steady with what is going on and to understand that you have a choice about what you do or do not do.

- Notice how you relate to objects. Do you pick up an instrument or unlock the front door of your home on autopilot? See if being more present changes these actions in a positive way.

- Every single small thing you do builds and attaches itself to a bigger whole. By paying careful attention to each act you perform, you are living in a loving manner.

- Do you really want to be happy? Just pay attention and be kind—unconditionally kind—during this breath alone. No matter what the circumstances, just be kind.

- Spiritual practice demands attention to your actions, even for the act of throwing out the garbage.

- Developing an integrated awareness of your entire being makes your body, your actions, your feelings, your relationships, your work, and your play all a part of your meditation.

- Do you argue or try to change people? Why? Because you are not content. But such actions will never bring contentment. Contentment only comes through patient, persevering effort plus insight.

- Practice noticing the immediate karma of your choices, like eating something you enjoy despite knowing that the food does not agree with you. Learn from this experience.

- You can break the pattern—change the next moment. You can do something different, enlightened, creative, imaginative, compassionate, wise, and fresh.

- Meditation is an adventure. Meditation is just to be—not doing anything.

- You might find yourself with two people around whom you normally behave differently. It's better to be yourself, as much as you can; otherwise, you'll find yourself walking on eggshells.

- You should practice nonviolence when interacting with a child, driving a car, or waiting for the shower water to warm up. Actions of impatience, inattentiveness, and negative judgment are considered "violent" actions in the context of Right Action.

- Real morality is based on a single criterion: Right Action, which is defined as the appropriate action in the present moment and present situation.

- In time, you will realize that everything you do is part of your practice.

- Remember and visualize the times in your life when you did good things for others. You are a giving, kind, compassionate person who deserves loving-kindness.

- We all feel worried at times, but if you feel like you are living in a constant state of unease, which sometimes heightens to overwhelming levels, take action. Meditate.

- Be satisfied with doing well, and do not worry about what others say.

- Witness your actions without judgment, to encourage nonattachment and compassion.

- You know your stories inside and out and backward and forward. Quit rehearsing these stories in your mind. Instead, enjoy the experience of the present moment.

- You burden yourself by thinking that happiness consists of having certain things or acting in a certain way. When you set aside these limited views, you will experience joy.

- Doing nothing requires vital energy. *Doing nothing* does not mean "laziness" or "passivity." It means doing nothing at all.

- Generate equanimity for others by reciting the following: All beings are the owners of their karma. Their happiness and unhappiness depend upon their actions, not my wishes for them.

- Bring attention to the act of choosing food.

- Become increasingly aware of the intentions that drive your actions. Sit with an intention for a while before deciding whether or not to follow through with it. Sense the feelings, the motivation, the decision to follow or not follow an intention. The more fully aware you are, the more you truly have a choice in acting or not acting on an intention.

- Do one thing at a time.

- Everything you do right now ripples outward and affects everyone.

- Do you need to make amends? Do you need to make some sort of change? Commit to any necessary actions to do both. Give thanks for what you have learned. Then ask yourself for forgiveness.

- Can you see how your choice of detergents, soaps, paper, and packaging affects the environment? This, too, is part of Right Action.

- Take your time with the food and drink that you consume. Take a sip and hold it in your mouth until you really notice the beverage's tastes and sensations. When you take a bite of food, chew it thoroughly, trying to identify each flavor, spice, and texture.

- Pay attention to strong sensations in the body—an itch, a pain. Observe the feeling as it is; do not grasp or reject it. The sensation will disappear by itself.

- Think about the best things you did during the last year. Use this evaluation to affirm your determination to carry on with good deeds.

- We often try to change the wrong person. If you want people to do more, you need to praise and appreciate what they are already doing for you.

- If you see that forsaking a lesser pleasure may bring a greater pleasure, be willing to do so. There's always a trade-off.

- Mindfulness does the job of massaging your internal formations, your blocks of suffering.

- The Buddha expressed the importance of the Middle Way regarding eating. Overeating numbs mindfulness. Moderation in eating is an important part of Right Action.

- Actions do speak louder than words, and your actions virtually shout when you are patient.

- It takes less energy to get an unpleasant task done now than to worry about it all day.

- Rather than acting automatically, don't scratch an itch until you have noted the intention to scratch it twice.

- Focus on the way you move and carry out simple tasks. Try to slow down everything you do, and be conscious of moving through space. Aim to do everything smoothly and gracefully.

- Benevolence is silent goodwill, streaming out indiscriminately into the world—into your life.

- Can you love without interfering? Can you love without imposing your will through manipulation or aggressive emotions and actions?

- You may feel remorse for doing something harmful. But hold the remorse in kindness; it is a gift you can give yourself.

- If you ate with mindfulness all the time, you would eat less and have more pleasant and satisfying experiences with food.

- Look at life like it is a blank canvas placed in front of you. Sit quietly until moved to action, then paint a picture.

- Follow the truth, forgive people, and act bravely.

- Cultivate the energy of mindfulness with mindful breathing and walking. Use these simple everyday acts to calm your emotions and nourish your joy.

- Whichever seeds you water will grow into plants. If you repeatedly act out of anger, you are watering the seeds of anger. If you meet your anger with kindness, then the loving seeds will grow.

- Even if you are hurrying, hurry mindfully. If you find your mind compelling you to get every last thing done, remind yourself that some of it can probably wait.

- Work toward seeing clearly what the skillful action is in every situation.

- Doing too many things at once disperses your energy. Focus on a specific task with full concentration.

- Doing something well and enjoying it is one of the finest experiences available to you—provided, of course, that you and others regard it as worthwhile.

- What you do, really do it—without dreading it, resenting it, or being thrilled by it.

- Any time you harm another through an intentional action, you harm yourself because you are creating the conditions for suffering and for repeating the action.

- Imagine that whoever you meet acts as they do solely for your benefit—to provide the teachings and difficulties you need in order to awaken. This may change your perspective.

- People who argue do not understand, and people who understand do not argue.

- Whenever possible, avoid eating in a hurry. Don't gobble up your food. Eating is an act of holiness. It requires full presence of mind.

- Imagine that the universe is about to whisper the answers to your deepest questions—and you do not want to miss them.

- Imagine yourself executing a performance perfectly from beginning to end. Practice this meditation several times before an actual performance.

- Doing anything you love with mindful awareness can be an effective meditation. Meditation is not the activity but the quality of attention that you bring to the activity.

- When you encounter someone who is suffering and you do not know how to help, imagine yourself in the other person's position. You may develop a clearer sense of how to help.

- If you're watching desire, wanting becomes the object of attention instead of the desire itself. The momentum that leads to an action to fulfill the desire will be dissipated.

- Commit for a period of time to pay close attention to your motivations and intentions. Keep asking yourself, Why? Do this for everything, from small to large actions. If you do something you do not feel good about, ask yourself why. If you do something you are proud of, ask yourself why.

- Be less bothered by the actions of others.

- A sense of well-being comes from not needing things. If you are constantly giving in to your impulse to do this or take that, you will never know what well-being is.

- Strive to avoid doing harm directly with your deeds or indirectly with your thoughts and intentions.

- Without awareness and respect, you simply repeat what was done to you, acting in ways conditioned by your own upbringing.

- Guilt is a purely negative emotion unless you use it as motivation to learn and change so that you act more responsibly in the present.

- Hold your seat. This means to stay centered—do not react. If something comes up, allow it to come and allow it to go. Hold your seat and see the illusions around you.

- Mindfulness is clear comprehension, paying attention to what you are doing, and knowing whether actions are skillful or unskillful.

- If happiness comes, don't become too excited. If suffering comes, don't become too depressed. Happiness and suffering are dependent upon your own mind and your own interpretation. They do not come from outside—from others.

- You learn something when you take responsibility for actions that are harmful, but you have to love yourself through that experience.

- If you can do something to make someone happy, do it right away. Anything you can do or say to make the person happy, say it or do it now. It is now or never.

- When an impulse arises, meditate on it, resolving not to do anything about it until it has arisen three times. By doing this you may discover a center of balance.

- Don't act like a self-appointed judge of your surroundings, as if you are judging an art contest or a beauty pageant.

- If there is just one person who is calm in a boat caught in a storm, this person can inspire calm in others. This person can save the whole boat. That is the power of nonaction.

- Whenever you are doing something and you want to do something else, stop, and for a short while simply exhale deeply and be in neutral gear. Then continue with the work. The work may go more quickly, and then you can move on to the next thing.

- Let the future take care of itself, under the approximate guidance of your own decisions and actions.

- Try this exercise to help you let go of control: spend a day doing nothing—absolutely nothing. Don't speak, don't watch television, don't listen to music, don't read, and eat little to nothing.

- Create an island of being in the sea of constant doing in which your life is usually immersed.

- Remember three essentials for happiness: something to do, someone to love, and something to hope for.

- Act on what is right in your own heart and there will be victory.

- If you are doing something, concentrate wholly on what you are doing. You can achieve this through the discipline that comes from meditation practice.

- Bad actions fill the pot slowly with great suffering.

- Practice mindful breathing so that the time spent washing the dishes is pleasant and meaningful.

- Just being, returning to original nature, is expanded consciousness. To do that, you have to become very quiet, very still.

- Feel sorrow or pain without resisting. Feel desire or dislike for someone or something without judging yourself for feeling driven to act on it.

- Pay attention—even in taking out the garbage—not only to what you discard but also to how you throw it away. An item may no longer be useful to you, but it is not useless.

- By learning to hold your mind to an object in meditation, you train in patience. Then when a moment of anger arises in everyday life, you may be able to prevent an unskillful reaction.

- Imagine that you are going to die in one minute. You may stop fighting, needing, wanting, and being concerned with physical comforts and achieving.

- The more natural that voluntary simplicity becomes, the easier it will be to do what is going to be good for others and what makes you happy. You may also find that your life becomes more consistent and fulfilling.

- Every morning before opening your eyes, stretch like a cat. After three or four minutes, begin to laugh. For five minutes, just laugh. Before long, laughing will be spontaneous and will change the nature of your whole day.

- It is impossible to move on to new states of mind unless you seek the forgiveness of those people you've offended.

- Have gratitude before eating, no matter how simple the meal. Appreciate the effort of all who labored to create it. Accept the meal as a means of attaining enlightenment.

- You may often find yourself taking refuge in things that you think are going to bring you happiness. They are not bad, but they do not bring lasting happiness.

- Make it your goal to carry out appropriate actions in an imperfect world.

- Offer this blessing to a person you know who is suffering: May you find peace. May you find healing. May you find happiness.

- If you keep doing what you've always been doing, then you'll keep getting what you've always been getting.

- When you clearly understand which of your actions cause happiness and which cause suffering, then you know how to find happiness and avoid suffering.

- Waiting means patience and silence. It means not being driven to action by your desires.

- Each time you take only your fair share, you are committing an act of generosity toward others.

- When you start to feel drowsy, acknowledge this. Do not use drowsiness as an object of attention; rather, find a different object, like the breath, and you will start to feel energized.

- Make a list of all that you have received today, even the small things. Make another list of all you have given. Make a third list of any trouble or pain you may have caused other people. This list making may teach you a great deal.

- To touch the present moment, you have to let the layer of concept drop away. When your mind stops racing, and you allow yourself to be in one place, you can be truly present.

- Every action brings an appropriate consequence to the doer. In your heart, you usually know how to behave. Listen to that inner voice. Sow good seeds and reap a good harvest.

- Pick one simple everyday action and use this one action to try to train yourself to be fully aware of what you are doing.

- Feel that you are bamboo, hollow and empty inside. Be with this feeling, and energy may suddenly start pouring into you.

- Live your life like a competent captain, setting a course and steering your boat when necessary while letting the wind and waves do most of the work.

- True mindfulness is an awareness that develops when your mind stays in contact with whatever you are doing.

- When you are irritated with someone, refrain from saying or doing anything. Instead, practice mindful walking, smiling, and breathing to restore your peace and calm.

- If you stay with the moment, there is just enough time to do what needs to be done, just enough materials to complete the job as far as it needs completing.

- If you are angry or in the middle of a strong emotion, stop and do nothing. Watch yourself. You have been caught in a momentary thunderstorm. Maintain stillness until it blows over.

- Consume with self-control, eating, drinking, and purchasing in moderation. Use only what you need.

- There is nothing that needs to be done about what arises in the mind. You can only control how you respond.

- The Middle Way, between indulgence and asceticism, is acknowledging the existence of the negative and then setting out to do something about it. The path to freedom from negativity has mindfulness as its foundation.

- Recognize children's suffering, and act with compassion to help them recognize anger, isolation, and fear. The energy of mindfulness can soothe and heal.

- The cause of all suffering is craving. Desire things that you do not have, and suffering will follow. If you realize this, peace will be yours.

- When you can be with whatever is happening in the moment, your sense of completeness will be present. You don't have to do anything about what is happening.

- Don't dwell upon the faults of others. If you do, your own faults get deeper.

- When you notice your mind wandering in the middle of an activity, try making an effort to come back to what is happening and to remain focused on the activity.

- Your mind makes everything. If you think something is difficult, it is difficult. When you do something, just do it.

- When you understand the confusion of the untrained mind, you won't look at ice cream and say, "That's happiness." You will realize that, because of its nature, the mind is content and happy.

- If you see anger clearly, it doesn't hurt anybody. It's when you get lost in anger or give it action that it hurts somebody.

- Do your work with an attitude of service. An attitude of service can transform even regular work into a spiritual practice.

- Use your meditation practice as a welcome oasis from doing, an opportunity to be without strategy or agenda. Play with a few meditation techniques, then choose one and stick with it.

- Mindful communication means being as clear and compassionate as possible. The tenet of mindful communication is nonharming: not engaging in any act that causes harm to yourself or others.

- Think of something you can do today to serve others selflessly.

- Living in the present means living at ease. Do not strain impossibly into the future.

- If you're constantly thinking about what you'd rather be doing, your mind is starved for mindfulness. If you do two unrelated things at once, you're not doing either of these things fully. You are missing out on your own life. The antidote is mindfulness.

- Every wakeful step and every mindful act is the path.

- It is better to say, "What I did was not very beneficial." There should be no self-hatred or sense of shame. Clearly assess what works and what does not.

- If you are present for your partner without expectation, grasping, attachment, or need, you are doing everything you can do.

- Become more loving and you will become more joyful. It does not matter whether you love a person, an animal, or a rock. The rock, animal, or person may not give anything in return, but that is not the point of love.

- People never stop saying and doing the wrong things, but it doesn't matter. The only thing that matters is to have peace and happiness in your own heart.

- To be in the here and now is a very positive contribution to life.

- Any time you feel it is easy to do so and you have the time, close your eyes and then inwardly stop. Just remain there. Suddenly, you will become aware that you are looking inside yourself.

- Watch for acts of beauty in yourself and others, and use them as inspiration.

- Good actions bring happiness, and bad actions bring misery. Good actions create good consequences.

- The simple person does not take himself too seriously. The simple person has no secrets, and he acts without guile, ulterior motives, agendas, or plans.

- Treat children with compassion, kindness, openness, and respect rather than seeing yourself as an authority separate from them.

- Instead of acting and reacting impulsively and following your thoughts and feelings here and there, watch your mind carefully, be aware, and try to deal skillfully with problems as they arise.

- To be idle is a short road to death, and to be diligent is a way of life; foolish people are idle, and wise people are diligent.

- Remember that when two opposite energies exist, they cancel each other out. Suddenly you have freedom. So, if you feel anger and you consciously seek to feel love, the anger will abate.

- Pay attention each time you change posture. Do you continually move in response to discomfort or pain, to relieve hunger, to scratch an itch, or to avoid boredom?

- Approach people with curiosity and know that each person has something to teach you. Seek the value in whatever each person does or says. Inwardly acknowledge these teachings.

- Complaints do nothing; a clearer, more direct request or suggestion may help alleviate a problem.

- Try one of these affirmations: I can do it. Let go. Peace forever. I am awake. I am joyful. I am free.

- Happiness depends on you alone. Happiness is constructed, and that requires effort and time.

- Hold in your mind the idea of happiness, and imagine yourself being happy from the inside out. To be happy, you must see yourself as happy.

- Experience your breath reflex as the thing that keeps you alive. Look at the source of that reflex as having the power compelling you to breathe.

- Look deeply into the interrelationship of all life and investigate your desires. You can then see if what you need is different from what you want.

- Pause before your emotions take over your actions.

- What happens to you does not matter; what you become through those experiences is all that is significant.

- See how comfortable, relaxed, free, and peaceful you feel when you act ethically.

- Always remember that whenever you are with a person, it may be the last time. Do not waste it with trivia, creating small troubles and conflicts that do not matter.

- Be kind, even to those whom you do not love. Be grateful to them for giving you the opportunity to do a kindness.

- To practice Right Action, you need to cultivate the self-discipline to not harm or act violently toward other beings.

- Read slowly and calmly so that the very act of reading is peace.

- The precepts involved with Right Action are founded on investigation—on bringing investigation to each moment by finding ways to manifest your intentions to do no harm.

- The best you can do is to help when you can, to witness others with kindness, to offer your presence, and to trust in life.

- During the day, you may encounter moments when you spontaneously feel love or compassion. Take time to close your eyes; meditate on the experience and allow it to deepen.

- Put wake-up cues on the bathroom mirror, on your car door or bedroom door, or on the stair banister: "May I remember to see what I am doing." "Do the action mindfully."

- Let yourself go. Drop all the anxieties of the day and allow yourself to sink into the peaceful pool of your quiet mind.

- Shopping often includes craving, creating a sense of self, and mindlessness. These things happen even during harmless impulse buying in the grocery store. Instead, bring mindfulness to the act of shopping.

- Becoming a more loving person in your everyday relationships may be one of the most compassionate actions you can do: becoming a little kinder.

- All of your thoughts and actions have an impact, first on you and then on those around you.

- You can decide not to get upset, anxious, or angry about things over which you have no power. You can choose to live your life with integrity, compassion, mindful observance, and a healthy sense of humor.

- Over time, a dripping tap will fill a pot with water. Over time, good actions will fill you with great happiness.

- Resentment only poisons your own heart while doing nothing to the intended target. Let it go.

- Be alert to flashes of unexpected beauty all around you—surprising acts of courage, compassion, wit, or wisdom from family and friends.

- Love means little if you pressure others to conform to your views of how they should be or what they should do.

- Recognize that all created things pass. What matters is not how much you collect or what you make or do, but how well you live this short dance and how well you learn to love.

- Believing what you think, especially that you have a separate self from others, leads to unskillful action.

- In harming another being, you harm yourself by rejecting interconnection with all life. You create bad karmic seeds that will cause you to harm again. If you yell at someone, you will likely yell at them again.

- Before your anger does injury to another, it actually does damage to you.

- Pick an activity that requires a lot of perseverance, and do it for a designated amount of time every day for a week. If you are not in the mood, do it anyway. See what happens to you and the activity as a result of this exercise.

- Always know why you're doing something. If there's no reason you can think of, it could be habit that's motivating you. Look at your actions and ensure that they're truly voluntary.

- Imagine yourself five years from now as you would most like to be, having done all the things you want to have done and having made all the contributions you want to have made. Now begin.

- It's all too easy to lose your patience with people and to act unkindly. A wise person knows that showing kindness and compassion is the most effective way to bring out the best in others.

- Refrain from re-enslaving yourself and stop getting caught up in pushing and pulling.

- Purposefully stop all the doing in your life and relax into the present without trying to fill it with anything.

- Imagine yourself at a crossroads. See the path that you have taken up to now. Do not judge, but see the path clearly. You cannot change that path, and there is no need to critique it. You can change direction now, so choose a new path.

- Notice craving—just see it. Don't act upon it, which is more craving, desiring an end to desire. The only way to eradicate craving is to see it and no longer feed it.

- Flowers grow on their own. Doing nothing is more than enough.

- While you are walking or sitting, or whenever you are not doing anything, exhale deeply. The emphasis of your breathing should be on the exhalation, and the longer the better.

- Self-confidence tends to slow people down, which for most of us would be highly desirable. When you are confident, you no longer need to prove yourself or be anxious about everyday encounters.

- Try saying "May I accept all things as they are. May I remain undisturbed by changing events."

- Whatever one does must emerge from an loving attitude for the benefit of others. (*The Life of Milarepa*)

- Make all of your actions throughout the day into meditation.

- If a behavior or a way of thinking does not have the positive payoff of making your life happy, it can and should be changed.

- Inject excitement into the precious time you spend with your partner by deliberately not planning what to do and where to go. Act on the spur of the moment.

- You are already complete, whole, and perfect. All of this action and effort to become special is only creating tremendous pain and suffering.

- It is an act of great kindness to learn how to let go in this life, to be with what is, to harmonize with life's changes, and to open to the mystery of the unknown.

- Asking yourself "What am I doing?" will help you overcome the habit of wanting to complete things quickly. Smile and say to yourself, "Washing this dish is the most important job in my life."

- What would you need to do and say to feel complete before you die, or to feel that you were dying in peace? If you really had a year to live, how would you change your life?

- Ambition and anger will disappear when you stop concerning yourself with the fruits of your actions.

- Each time you act with compassion toward another, you are committing an act of generosity.

- Practicing what you preach applies to love as well as to moral virtues; it's easier to say the words than to act on them. Express your love in action and thought.

- Happiness is confidence that pain and disappointment can be tolerated, that love will prove stronger than aggression. Happiness is release from the attachment to pleasant feelings. It is the realization that you do not have to be so self-obsessed.

- Act in positive ways and let go of misery.

- Imagine that you are watching every aspect of your behavior on television. Preempt embarrassment by acting well now.

- With loved ones, the best approach is to simply stop and gather awareness to act more skillfully, more appropriately, and with consideration for all involved.

- Think of the very center of your being as the center of a cyclone or tornado. Whatever happens around it does not affect it. It is silent and calm.

- If you understand the present moment, it guides how you act and what you choose to do.

- What you do and how you act creates your future experiences.

- Improve your karma by reframing how you respond. Let a challenging situation go, and balance your actions. Don't dwell on the situation or complain about it, especially because the situation will change and dissipate.

- Observe or witness a desire to act with a sense of detachment, as though you are watching a play.

- The things you do should lead to dispassion, disentangling, the dispersion of the causes of suffering, wanting little, contentment, and peaceful solitude.

- Imagine rowing down a river. Trying to stay in the middle is hard because of the crosscurrents. Let the boat drift, instead of steering it, and enjoy the experience. Take this attitude into daily life and try to release the need to control things.

- Think of the chores you face in the day ahead as a privilege, not a burden. Resolve to enjoy the satisfaction of doing them to the best of your ability. Take pleasure in your skills.

- You cannot escape aging, physical degeneration and sickness, or death. Only your karma accompanies you after death; karma is the ground on which you build your life.

- Learn how to fully acknowledge who you are and what you do. Then, let these things go.

- Try not to rehearse a dialogue or anticipate what a person is going to say. Don't go into a conversation with your mind made up and ears and heart closed.

- If you are on the shore of suffering, anger, and depression and want to cross to the shore of well-being, practice mindful breathing, look at these feelings, and smile. By doing these things, you cross over.

- Have the strength of patience and tolerance, and do not become overwhelmed by adverse situations or conditions.

- Eating in moderation can be a committed spiritual practice. Each time you feel hunger is an opportunity for you to examine your relationship with craving, clinging, and taking.

- It is not doing the thing you like to do but liking the thing you have to do that makes life blessed.

- Mindfulness simply knows what is happening—it does not judge, does not try to push away, and does not cling.

- Take a habit you want to break, and turn it into a meditation. When you do the habit, pay close attention to every sensation and feeling involved. Don't focus on stopping or changing the habit. The next time you indulge the habit, see what has changed.

- Act to promote harmony and unity. Refrain from allowing your attachments and expectations to cause or further an argument.

- Decision-making is often hard. Let action flow naturally from your resolve. If you have to wait before embarking on the choice, reaffirm your trust in yourself.

Essays

Anger

Just before you show anger in action or speech, pause and think about what you are about to do. The pause is vital to taking a wise look at the possible consequences and reactions. Pausing is especially helpful if you are going to say or write something. If you lash out in anger, the person you are wanting to communicate with may walk away or not write back, and you will be left in a place where you know that expressing your anger did not alleviate the problem.

Pausing lets you see that there is nothing gained from getting angry. You can smile to your ignorance and breathe out. Letting go is the better way to deal with anger. Since very few people—even when confronted—admit they are wrong, by not confronting them you relieve yourself of having to deal with a situation that could cause you more suffering or anger. Letting go of anger and not confronting others is a preventative exercise, because by doing so you do not have to expend the time and energy that is necessary to repair the damage that your anger might have caused.

Uproot anger by acknowledging it as a state of mind, by naming it, and by giving it space. Shine the light of awareness on anger, and it will lose its hold over you. Feeling and showing compassion is the better response.

Attention

Whenever you can do just one simple thing, be in that moment. Think of that moment as a one-pointed concentration. "Zen is not some kind of excitement, but concentration on usual everyday routine," said Shunryu Suzuki.

You have the ability to pay attention to everything with equal fervor. But you can train yourself to pay more attention. This state of hyperfocus is sometimes called *immovable wisdom*, and it means focusing on an unmoving center but retaining fluidity in your focus, so that your mind is clear and ready to direct its attention wherever it may be needed.

Meditation is the practice Buddha taught to develop attention. In meditation, your anchor, or focus, is the breath, and each time your mind wanders, you bring it back to the breath. Working with instead of struggling against the resistance of your mind builds inner strength and deepens concentration and attention.

Practice meditation by creating "flow" experiences with an activity you love, paying attention to what is happening and learning to enjoy the immediate experience. The moment you give close attention to anything, even a blade of grass, it becomes a mysterious, awesome, indescribable, and magnificent world in and of itself.

Aversion

Aversion is one of the three afflictions, or poisons, said Buddha. (The others are attachment and ignorance.) Aversion manifests itself as anger, revulsion, hatred, dislike, fear, and even indifference. Resistance to change is a major indication that aversion may be playing a role in your life. When you feel aversion, it is probably related to the things that you find unpleasant, try to avoid, or cause you suffering. We need to remember that pain is part of life, but suffering is optional.

Practice embracing the reality of a situation without aversion. The first step is awareness. If you are experiencing the disturbing feelings that are a form of aversion, you can contemplate or meditate on them. One way to deal with aversion is to breathe in the burden, accepting it, and then breathe out goodness to others. Awareness of how you experience aversion can help you transform those experiences to ones of loving-kindness and compassion. This awareness and transformation is a new, good habit you can develop through meditation.

Feelings of aversion come and go, just like the people, states, or situations that we find unpleasant. Pushing things away, mentally or physically, does not offer relief. Instead, work toward recognizing your aversions, acknowledge them, and try to smile and let go. As you do these things, you can also let the aversions go without getting caught up in them. Become aware of how much negative time and energy you spend on your feelings of dislike and distaste. By practicing letting them go, you may open yourself up to all kinds of extra time and energy to do the things that make you happy. And by developing a joyous state of mind, you will decrease aversion.

Awareness

Awareness is a skill that you can develop through mindfulness. Awareness is the difference between stopping to smell the roses and not even seeing the roses. You can transform routine activities and chores into meditation by establishing and maintaining awareness while doing them. And when you bring awareness into any situation, it can help you improve your ability to be patient—to understand and put things in perspective.

In meditation, you are training your awareness on whatever arises within your mind. What does this mean? It means that you can see these mind states, but you do not identify with them. When you notice these mind states, bring your attention back to your breath and the mind will become calm and your focus sharper.

Awareness means stopping to look at one thing or doing one thing at a time. Practice doing one thing at a time consciously, slowly, and with awareness and respect. If you are present in your thoughts and actions and fully inhabit each moment, you will find a flow and rightness to whatever you do. Every action will be as it should be. If you do every little thing with mindful awareness, you will be living Zen.

Balance

We live in a very busy and noisy world, and as adults we often feel funny letting play into our lives. Play is needed to balance life, whether you are a child (whose "work" is school) or an adult. Play makes you appreciate work and vice versa. Of course, the best of all possible worlds is to feel that the universe is your playground. How could anything be more fun than loving what you do and feeling that it matters?

The Buddha promoted a balanced approach to life, the Middle Way. This balance starts with your mind and continues on to your impulses and behavior. The elements in life that require the most balancing can be divided into "internal" and "external." Oftentimes, people focus on one more than the other. For example, you may find that you focus on external things—like work, relationships, and activities—and pay very little attention to what is going on inside your heart and mind. Or maybe you spend so much time being self-reflective that sometimes you miss out on the experience of living.

Don't overlook opportunities to play. Watch how little children play and learn from them. Do puzzles if you like them, or draw in a sketchbook. Annotate your books with comments and opinions. Change your exercise to be more playful; instead of cycling by yourself, join a group ride. You can become more playful simply by doing what you like to do and not apologizing for it. Even spending fifteen minutes reading a gossip magazine can be an indulgence that gives you pleasure.

Change and Impermanence

Change and impermanence are the essential characteristics of all phenomena. You cannot say of anything, animate or inanimate, organic or inorganic, "This is lasting." Because even as you say this, the entity is undergoing change. All is fleeting: the beauty of flowers, the bird's melody, the bee's hum, and a sunset's glory.

The same man cannot step twice into the same river, for man is only a combination of mind and body and does not remain the same for two consecutive moments, and a river is composed of constantly shifting and flowing molecules. Viewing things as they really are is seeing the impermanent, unsatisfactory, and no-self nature of all things.

History has proved again and again—and will continue to prove—that nothing is lasting. Nothing can be clung to, grasped, or held on to. Everything lives and dies, comes and goes; everything changes and is impermanent. Accepting change and impermanence brings you happiness.

Cleaning

Organizing clutter, cleaning out trash, and donating unused items to those who could use them can bring much happiness. Make a list of all the places you could clean out, both physical and mental. Cleaning is not carried out to make room for more stuff; rather it is a cleansing, detoxing, and simplifying exercise.

A key ingredient to living a happier life is to simplify it. When you see all the stuff that you are cleaning out, you will be amazed at how much was purchased that you did not need. Be generous in giving things away that you truly will never use again (for example, clothes, books, old linens, dishes, sporting goods, and appliances). Donate items to worthy causes and take time to understand how much you are enriching someone else's life with your gifts.

If cleaning seems like a boring chore to you, try doing it as a form of meditation. Put your entire mind into the task, concentrate, and do it slowly and completely. Take a chore and imagine you're doing it for the first time. Look for the bubbles in the sink full of dirty dishes. Use your five senses, focusing on one at a time. Appreciate the warmth of the water and the scent of the dishwashing liquid. Incorporating mindfulness into everyday life can make you calmer and make your mind more adaptive.

Compassion

"Compassion brings us to a stop, and for a moment we rise above ourselves." This great quote by Mason Cooley says a lot about the importance of compassion. When we experience compassion, it is truly one of the gifts of life. In life we meet people that we just do not like or who say things we don't like. We may even feel that we hate or despise a person. Developing compassion for such people can set you free.

Meditation is the place to cultivate compassion. Try this: Breathe and smile a half smile. Envision the person who has caused you the most suffering. Contemplate the features of this person that you hate or despise the most or find the most repulsive. Try to examine what makes this person happy and what causes this person suffering. Contemplate the person's perceptions; try to see the patterns of thought and reason that this person follows. Examine what motivates this person's hopes and actions. Continue all of these steps until you feel compassion rise in your heart and your anger and resentment disappear.

Practice this exercise regularly until you are able to let go of hatred or dislike. You will experience true freedom when you can master this, and you will be able to carry compassion over to many other areas of your life.

Control

One thing that distinguishes human beings from other animals is our ability and desire to look toward the future. We spend a great deal of our life imagining what it would be like to be this way or that way, to do this or that, to taste or buy or experience some thing or state or feeling. Each of us could compile a list of "if only" things—if only I had, was, could do.

How good have you been at predicting the impact of attaining these "if only" things? Have you found that your imagination is not very accurate? Did you really feel the way you thought you would when you attained some object, goal, or job? Or did you replace that earlier desire or craving with a whole new list? It is important to see what always wanting more and always desiring to control your life does to you.

The Buddha taught that through meditation and mindfulness, we do have control over what we think about our experiences, and therefore we also have control over how we feel about those experiences and how we respond to them. The Buddha taught that even when a situation is not in our control, our reaction to it is.

Notice your need for control, whether it be over people, politics, your body, your mind, your past, your future, or even the weather. Try to observe this desire rather than getting caught up in it. Note any thoughts you have about what you believe "should be." Soften and relax negative feelings about not being in control. Once you have your mind under control, you can sit in full awareness, noticing thoughts and feelings but not engaging or judging—simply being. Recognize what you can control, and let go of what you cannot.

Deeds

Explore each of these precepts for a week and see how your relationship changes toward each one:

- Purposefully bring no harm in thought, word, or deed to any living creature. Become particularly aware of any living beings in your world whom you ignore, and cultivate a sense of care and reverence for them, too.

- Act on every single thought of generosity that arises spontaneously in your heart.

- Do not gossip (positively or negatively) or speak about anyone who is not present. Do not criticize others or yourself in your mind either.

- Observe meticulously how often sexual feelings and thoughts arise in your consciousness. Each time, note what particular mind states are associated with thoughts, such as aggression, caring, compulsion, desire for communication, greed, loneliness, love, pleasure, tension, and so on.

- Refrain from all intoxicants and addictive substances (even caffeine). Observe the impulses to use these substances, and become aware of what is going on in your heart and mind at the time of the impulses.

What have you learned? As you practice these precepts more and more, you will see that you are able to apply what you have learned to various areas of your life.

Delusion and Ignorance

From the Buddhist point of view, the unwillingness or failure to see the facts of life as they are, to see ourselves as we are, and to conduct ourselves in harmony with these realities, are the chief causes of our self-inflicted suffering and, therefore, the chief obstacles to happiness. The state of denial, or the lack of realization of the facts of existence, is often termed "ignorance." One of the Buddha's great contributions to the world was the realization that ignorance is the primary cause of the sufferings we impose on ourselves and others.

Ignorance is equivalent to the identification of a self as being separate from everything else. Ignorance consists of the belief that there is an "I" that is not part of anything else. Each of us thinks, *I am one and unique. Everything else is not me, but something different.* This identification creates a dualistic view of "me" and "others." This, then, creates two opposite reactions to many of the things life presents us: "This is nice—I want it!" and "This is not nice—I do not want it!"

The antidote to ignorance is the development of awareness and wisdom, both of which are achieved by training in the ways of the Eightfold Path, especially in investigating the mind through meditation. The antidote is understanding that everything and everyone is interconnected and everything and everyone changes.

Desire and Attachment

Suffering is a part of all our lives, but the amount we suffer is actually optional. You may believe in your attachments and desires as well as your aversions and hates. But you may also see how wanting that coat or that pint of ice cream turns into suffering when you realize that each was an indulgence you could not afford or that brought you nothing more than a few moments of happiness. After you answer a craving or desire, how often do you move on to a new craving or desire? Desire and attachment constitute a hamster wheel that you'd be better off dismounting.

Everything changes and is impermanent. Even the states of desire and attachment change. What you wanted a week ago may no longer interest you. When your favorite cup breaks, you may be upset for a brief time, but then you get over it and possibly become attached to the cup you buy to replace the broken one.

The Buddha taught that seeing oneself as separate from people, things, or experiences is a delusion. It is a delusion that is the deepest cause of our unhappiness. We "pursue" happiness because we think it comes from outside of us. But it's also true that because we think things are outside of us we become stressed about them and worry about them. We may go through life grabbing one thing after another to ease our stress and worry. We may attach not only to physical things but also to ideas and opinions about ourselves and the world around us.

By practicing the Eightfold Path, we can realize the true nature of "self" and "other" and put an end to desire and attachment. Seeing through the delusion of separation means you do not give external things any power. You seek equanimity, to be free from the compulsion to chase what you want. Seeing through desire and attachment is a life practice, not a quick fix. It is a practice that requires giving up ideas about goals and rewards or of escaping to a better place.

Distraction

Investigate your distractions and mind clutter. Be an observer. Do not try to describe them or react or judge. A distraction is just a distraction. If a distracting thought or series of thoughts bombards you, acknowledge the distraction and then let the thought or thoughts go.

Spend some time reflecting on what the distractions are in your life. What activities or habits do you participate in or have in order to avoid doing projects or avoid being with yourself? Do you work way too much or always say yes to what friends and family members ask of you? Do you eat to distract yourself? Surf the Internet and and interact with social media?

When you are upset, do you eat cookies? Why? To feel more "full"? Are you afraid of being alone with yourself? Why are you afraid of being alone? Seek out some of the underlying thoughts or beliefs behind the distractions you create.

For one week, just notice yourself when you engage in distractions. Sit and be with these emotions, working toward no longer needing to distract yourself from the parts of life that you don't like.

By meditating and training yourself to do nothing, you may find that your mind gets better at immersing itself in an activity. You may find that you are less plagued by distractions, desires, and fragmentation.

Doing One Thing at a Time

Have you ever heard this proverb? "One thing at a time, and that done well, is a very good thing, as any can tell." Doing one thing at a time seems unusual in our multitasking world. Multitasking is like splitting the brain to do different things.

When you brush your teeth, really feel the toothbrush on every tooth. When you fold the laundry, smooth each item and fold it carefully. When you tie your shoes, look at the knot as you create it. Being aware of doing one thing at a time is a very comforting experience. You may find that as you do one thing at a time more often, you feel more confident completing tasks that are more complicated.

Productivity isn't just about getting through a task; it should also be about completing the task to some level of quality. Rushing through a task quickly so you can declare that it's "complete" isn't productivity, because someone will have to clean up the mess later—probably you. The fact is that most of us aren't getting much done, nor are we experiencing the satisfaction of completing each task—especially not with any quality or thought—because we are multitasking. Focus on one thing at a time and let the imperfections of life be.

Eating and Drinking

To eat in a mindful way, you should fully and completely taste every bite and crumb. If you are present in your eating, you can't binge. You may find more enjoyment in healthful foods. And if you savor every bite of chocolate or every french fry, you won't need as much. Though we eat to nourish our bodies, we taste food to satiate our minds. The brain feasts on the aroma and flavor of each mindful bite and sip we bring to our mouths long before the stomach is part of the process.

Eating mindfully requires great concentration. Think of how often you spent an hour preparing a dinner that everyone ate in five minutes! Marcel Proust showed the world this with his story of the madeleine cake. In his novel *Swann's Way*, the narrator of the story experiences an awakening upon truly and thoroughly tasting a madeleine cake. You can probably intuitively understand how savoring food and drink is a whole different, and happier, experience than gulping down something without taking the time to explore all of its features.

When you eat or drink something, first take it in with your eyes and nose. Take a small bite or sip and move it around in your mouth. Savor it. Put the utensil or glass down. Sense what type of taste you're experiencing. Fully chew if it is food, and then enjoy the swallowing. Notice the impulse to take another bite before the first one has been chewed and swallowed. Be with every aspect of the ingesting experience. Give thanks for each taste and those to come. Continue to eat and drink as slowly as you can, with mindfulness.

Envy and Jealousy

It is possible to unlearn jealousy. Jealousy indicates that you don't like something about yourself. It may seem to be directed toward others, but your jealousies point back to you and what you feel are your shortcomings, weaknesses, faults, and disappointments. Jealousy is also concerned with the fear of losing something you possess. Jealousy is not love of another; it indicates a focus on self-love, which corrodes the heart and actually makes you feel ugly.

To cure jealousy is to see it for what it is: a dissatisfaction with yourself that is all in your mind. The mind is something you can control. Since you are not your thoughts, you are also not your jealous thoughts. See this unskillful mind state for what it is, and let it go.

"Jealousy," as defined in Buddhism, covers part but not all of the English word "envy." In its definition, *envy* also includes "covetousness," the inordinate desire for something that someone else possesses. Envy is a painful or resentful awareness of an advantage enjoyed by someone else joined with the desire to enjoy the same advantage. If we are envious and want even more, our covetousness has grown into greed, which can develop into spite.

Envy, as a combination of jealousy and covetousness, leads to competitiveness. Being jealous and envious of what others have accomplished, we may push ourselves or others to do more and more, as seen in extreme competition in business or sports.

When—through study and meditation—you stop the dualistic thinking of "me" and "others," you can do away with the disturbing emotions of jealousy and envy.

Ethics and Morality

When you follow the Eightfold Path, you are observing Buddhist ethics. When you study the precepts of not harming and not killing, you must consider such topics as abortion, capital punishment, euthanasia, vegetarianism, and—with the topic of sexual misconduct—affairs, casual sex, and other such issues.

To live is to act, and our actions can have either harmful or beneficial consequences for ourselves and others. Buddhist ethics are concerned with the principles and practices that help one to act in ways that help rather than harm. The core ethical code of Buddhism is based on the Five Precepts being put into practice with intelligence and sensitivity.

From the Buddhist point of view, these precepts are guidelines to Right Action. They are an essential part of Buddhist training and a fundamental means to purification. Especially in the context of the practice of meditation, the training precepts prevent destructive actions. By following the precepts, you remove greed, hatred, delusion, guilt, anxiety, and restlessness.

To be ethical and moral, focus on what is skillful and unskillful and proceed along those lines. The Buddhist precepts are an invitation to explore how your life can change as you take on certain ethical challenges.

Feelings

What is joy to you? We often associate joy with the things and events in our lives that produce warm feelings of pleasure, but true joy requires no external stimuli. It is a state of mind that exists no matter what is happening around you. If you try, you can reflect inner joy in your life and work. And bringing joy to others feeds your own happiness, too. You can start by bringing joy to family members and friends and then extend it to others.

We also face bad news, unpleasant feelings, and true hardship. Like death and taxes, these feelings are inevitable in life. In what ways have these events made you wiser? What have you overcome? Did any of these situations help you become more tolerant of others, more patient, or more content with your life?

By accepting the directions your life takes—good or bad, within or outside of your control—you can accept life, truth, and reality. Think about the times when something bad happened that eventually revealed itself as a blessing, or a time when you got something you really, really wanted and then found it had a negative impact. Things always change, but you can resolve to see your feelings for what they are and work to remain in a calm center, where you aren't buffeted about by feelings.

Generosity

Doing things for others is only Right Action if there is no expectation of thanks or reward or recognition. If you give a gift with the expectation that the receiver will think you are great, you are not giving an unselfish or a thoughtful gift. Helping someone with the hope of accolades is not a kindness at all. Happiness is not found in these ways.

We may focus too much on ourselves at times. Practicing generosity is an impulse of the heart. True generosity is guided by awareness. It is a giving that is not dictated by a sense of guilt, by a debt, by wanting to show off, or by wanting to create dependence. Generosity is truly a free gift, which generates freedom. This feeling of freedom even exists when you are generous to yourself.

Studies have found that happier people tend to be generous. If you are more content, you are likely to be kinder to others. Someone who feels gratification is more apt to feel generous and to help another in difficulty. Generosity is a mood lifter. So, think about how you would like to be more generous to your family, your community, and the world. Actively look for more opportunities to give your time, energy, money, goods, love, or service to others.

Goal Setting

What is a goal? A goal is the basic unit of life design. Determining what your goals are can be a difficult process. It is easy to dream, but if you want to make a dream come true, you have to start by making a plan. A plan has concrete steps, a start date, and an end date. No goal is set in stone, and the plan can be changed. Remember that goals exist to serve you and make you happy.

Let's say you choose a goal that is important to you. Diagram the steps as you know them. Are you ready to take the first step? If so, take that first step and see whether it feels skillful and right. Goals can also be something we cling to inappropriately, and we might end up giving ourselves a hard time when we don't meet them. Grasping and clinging cause suffering. So when setting goals, you have to watch out for these hindrances and figure out ways to let go of expectations.

If you don't look at goals as expectations, you won't beat yourself up when you don't achieve them. Hold your goals lightly so they represent the direction in which you want to move rather than something you must achieve. If you do this, you won't obsess about progress and you will be able to accept that change is messy and unpredictable. Accept that you have to start from where you are right now. Accept the present moment, because anything good that comes from achieving a goal is the result of acceptance.

Harmful Speech

A little reflection will show that speech and the written word can have enormous consequences. Speech can break lives, create enemies, and start wars, or it can give wisdom, heal divisions, and create peace.

If you say what's true for you, and say it clearly and kindly, you get one kind of result. But if you use a sharp tongue, speak falsely, exaggerate, or raise your voice, you get a different result: unnecessary conflict, a lost opportunity, a tightness in your chest, and so on.

It is important to pay attention not only to what you say but why, when, and how you say it. Look at the state of mind that precedes what you say, the motivation for your comments and responses. Ask yourself what it is like for people who are subject to your speech. How would you feel if someone said the same thing to you? Put yourself in the other person's shoes. Before you speak, ask yourself, Is this kind? Is it necessary? Is it true? Does it improve upon silence?

Harming or Killing

Making peace and walking a peaceful path supports happiness. If you aren't at peace, happiness is almost impossible. It is easy to get mad and angry—to let your negative and hurtful emotions get the best of you. A path of peace requires awareness, restraint, and attention.

The first step on the peaceful path is to see the good in other people. By training yourself to do this, you create an energy in yourself that is very powerful. Give others and yourself the benefit of the doubt. Your life is a gift. Enjoy that gift by treating yourself and others with respect.

Reduce violence in your actions. The precept of not killing—not physically harming another being—has many facets, from dealing with insects and mice to capital punishment. By following the precept, you are trying to develop compassion that is undiscriminating and all-embracing. You aim to see the world as a unified whole in which each thing or creature has its place and function. We should each strive to develop a little more respect for life. And this is what the precept of not killing—the first precept—is saying.

See how much you can refrain from harming in your life, knowing that the extent to which you are willing to go may change and evolve as you proceed along the peaceful path.

Intention

To understand karma, it is essential to see how the motivation, or intention, preceding an action determines the result of that action. If an act is motivated by true kindness, it will bring a positive result. If an act is motivated by aggression or greed, it will eventually bring an unpleasant result. Because karmic results do not always bear fruit immediately, it is sometimes difficult to observe this process.

Karma can be seen in a fairly direct way through your actions. Take two to three days to carefully notice the intentions that motivate your actions. Direct your attention to the state of mind that precedes the doing of a deed. Try to be particularly aware of whether your act is even subtly motivated by boredom, compassion, competitiveness, concern, fear, greed, irritation, loneliness, or love. Be aware, too, of the general mood or state of your heart and mind and how those things may be influencing what you do.

Try to observe without any judgment. Simply notice the various motivations in the mind. Then notice the effect of the action you took. What response did it elicit? In discovering the power of your inner states to determine outer conditions, you will be able to follow a path that can more often lead to genuine happiness.

Karma

Karma means "You don't get away with nothing" (Ruth Denison), that everything you think, do, or say has an effect. The consequence of an action, thought, or word may not instantly be evident, but it undeniably will come, and there is no escaping personal responsibility for what you consciously think, do, and speak. Karma is cause and effect: what you do today, good or bad, comes back to you tomorrow. Your thoughts, your words, and your deeds create the experience that is your future.

In order to understand karma, you must constantly remind yourself that every action has a consequence. You must take the time to consider whether what you are about to do, say, or even think may be beneficial or harmful. You can break bad patterns and habits; you can change the next moment. You can do something different, enlightened, creative, imaginative, compassionate, and wise. You can transform your existence and that of those around you.

Look at the present circumstances of your life and ask, "What can I do right now to create good karma?"

Kindness

Treat yourself the way you would treat a child you love very much. With the child, you would be patient and kind. You would be helpful. You might indulge, but you would know when to say no. You can offer yourself this same kindness. You have to generate love and compassion for yourself first before offering it to others—like first putting on your oxygen mask on an airplane and then assisting your seatmates. The nourishment that comes from being kind to yourself is the kind of food that stays with you and that you can share.

Be as kind as possible to yourself and those around you. There is an inextricable relationship between happiness and kindness. Just be kind, right now. No matter the circumstances, be kind. Whether you're with a family member, a friend, a lover, someone on the street, someone who seems to hate you, or little old you, just be kind in whatever way is appropriate.

To be kind, it helps to recall times when someone was kind to you—small acts or large ones. Focus on the details. Remember how appreciative you were. Remember how good you felt and how many times you have told the story surrounding the act.

Practicing kindness gives us happiness. The more you treat yourself and others well, the happier you will feel. Kindness is the starting point, the fount from which flows so many other positive qualities, such as forgiveness, generosity, honesty, and patience. For your life to be of value, you need to foster and nurture compassion and kindness.

Likes and Dislikes

Very simply, sorting all phenomena into "like" or "dislike" bins gets in the way of enlightenment. The Buddha said that to be free we must first understand the unreal nature of all the things in our minds, such as likes and dislikes. But the subject of judgments is subtle, and the path of peace is found in the practice of equanimity, or nonattachment.

Having likes and dislikes is a given; indeed, the ability to discriminate is considered an essential part of what makes us human beings. After all, human beings, unlike other living creatures, can form judgments and make choices. Free will and choice are taken as fundamental rights. So, what's the problem with having likes and dislikes?

The problem occurs when our likes and dislikes become solidified in our minds as inflexible opinions and truths. When we form negative judgments about ourselves and other human beings, these judgments become the lenses through which we view and experience ourselves and the world around us. You can probably see that this causes harm and suffering, both for ourselves and for others.

Likes and dislikes easily can pull you off the Buddha's path. If you follow what you like, that's craving and attachment. If you believe in your dislikes, you may feel fear and aversion. The Buddha wants each of us to walk freely between attraction and aversion, likes and dislikes, and praise and blame without attaching to one side or the other, and without being jerked this way or that. Use meditation to see likes and dislikes as unimportant judgments you create in your mind. Accept them and don't judge (that's another like or dislike!), and let go of them as much as possible.

Listening

Listening is an important part of the precept of Right Speech. We should cultivate an equal amount of listening and silence to balance our talking and writing.

Our brains pick up all types of information, even from nonverbal clues. But a major portion of what we think we just heard is the product of our imagination. Without realizing it, when listening to others we fill in the gaps in our understanding with our own thoughts instead of really listening to their words in the moment.

Mindful listening is giving others your full attention. Let yourself open up to the words that are coming toward you. Concentrate on every word being said. Still your mind and open your heart to fully hear the other person. Concentrate: do not be distracted by your own thoughts and emotions. Hear the other person with acceptance and compassion.

A mindful listener will find that her communications are much happier. Not saying anything when you have nothing beneficial, useful, or skillful to say will prove you to be wise. The real practice of listening is to focus on the experience itself rather than on what you perceive. Bathe in the sounds around you and find a point of silence within. Just listen.

Love

What is your definition of love? Is there more than one kind of love? It can't hurt to expand your idea of love. Love is clearly part of happiness. It is probably the most powerful emotion we feel. True happiness is unselfish love that increases in proportion as it is shared. To have love be part of happiness, we have to think of love beyond romantic terms and even beyond the family. You can look at love in a spiritual way, too.

A happy life, for most, includes genuine friendships and lasting bonds to others. A happy life involves opening your heart to care for and about others. If you restrict your definition of love, then you could be missing out—because in loving and being loved, you reach down into the enlightened being inside yourself. Love is true joy. In the end, nothing you do or say in this lifetime will matter more than how much you have loved.

Sit by a rock and have a chat. Stroke the rock and feel at one with it. The rock may not return anything, but that is not the point of love. You become joyful because you loved that rock. And if you can do this with a rock, it is easy to move on to sentient beings.

Love the people in your life by acting in harmonious ways, by bringing awareness to your behavior, and by acting with integrity. Love them as you would like to be loved. It is a simple rule to follow that has powerful results. Can you love without interfering? Can you love without imposing your will through manipulation or aggressive emotions and actions? Open up and love—today.

Mindfulness

You can redefine "spiritual life" as your day-to-day life lived with intention and integrity. Every routine thing, from brushing your teeth to resolving a conflict to shoveling the snow, can be part of your spiritual practice. Instead of going through these things on autopilot, in an impersonal way, make daily activities personal—really be there. You can construct a spiritual life from the everyday stuff. Instead of feeling like you don't have time for spirituality, you make the business of everyday living into a spiritual life.

Paying acute attention to each happening, each action, and each word is called "mindfulness." Each twenty-four-hour period is a gift of human life. But often it may seem to get away from you. Using mindfulness, none of this time will get away from you, but mastering this focus takes practice. It's so easy to go on autopilot, especially because autopilot seems to save you time, but that is simply not true. When you are on autopilot, you are not in the moment, and you often forget things, bobble things, and do other things that actually cost you time. And because you were not in the moment, you actually threw the time away.

As you practice mindfulness during everyday activities, you will breathe more deeply and see more wonders. You will likely become more insightful, more content, and maybe more trusting.

When you practice mindfulness, even the most mundane things—walking, driving, working, and caring for others—can become a new challenge. When you pay attention and become mindful, you may marvel at the simple things in life that you once passed over. These ordinary things are part of the journey of life, and you will find added happiness when you start to notice them through the practice of mindfulness.

Moderation and Abstention

The Buddhist precepts encourage moderation, abstention, and self-control. Buddhism encourages a sense of self-identity based not upon desires, but upon self-fulfillment and self-respect—a self-respect that seeks to do no harm. Buddhism also encourages love, compassion, equanimity, and a harmless lifestyle. Buddhism teaches moderation in all things.

Look for ways you can pull back a bit in life and moderate your behavior. Points of unhappiness in your home, work, and even leisure time may indicate an imbalance that you can correct. Moderation and balance lead toward peace and equanimity. You can be really involved in your career, but if your family feels neglected and you have no hobbies, you and your loved ones may suffer. In situations like these, it may help to ask yourself if moderation and balance in what you do and how you spend your time would benefit you.

Abstention falls into all five of the Buddhist precepts: abstaining from taking life, abstaining from doing harm, abstaining from stealing, abstaining from telling lies and other harmful speech, and abstaining from taking intoxicants to the point that they affect your behavior. Abstention serves the purpose of cleansing your life of action that is unskillful. It may sound extreme, but it is really just a way of practicing moderation.

Nonviolence

In Buddhism, nonviolence is an important precept, and it actually encompasses far more than physical violence. Negativity is a form of violence. When someone asks you a simple question and you snap back with a nasty response, that is an act of violence.

Be aware of negative actions, emotional states, intentions, and mental and physical reactions. It is easier for us to witness negative reactions in other people than in ourselves. You may often justify your own negative reactions, but they are not skillful or beneficial. Learning to recognize and then accept old, conditioned negative emotional reactions are the first steps to changing these reactions, which leads to a nonviolent existence.

Practice nonviolence by looking for the good in everything. Also practice it by noticing when a negative thought arises: observe it without judgment before replacing it with a positive thought or simply letting it go.

We also add violence to our lives through the Internet, television, movies, and video games. How does watching a horror movie or a television news report about a killing spree make you feel? How does reading snarky social media comments or hearing swear words in a movie make you feel? These are forms of violence that we can work to avoid by more carefully choosing what media we let into our lives and how we let it in.

Openness and Belonging

The sense of belonging is a basic need, and it is part of the answer to one of life's major questions: Who am I? You belong to a family, a group, a society, and a profession, and these affiliations define you and give you reasons for existing. Without this belonging, you would feel like nothing.

We live in an era of individualism that celebrates being "special." People valued the sense of community and belonging more in the past. We need to cultivate these sensibilities in the present, and not just online. Anything we can do to strengthen the sense of community and move away from isolation is worthwhile. While people are certainly more connected to each other electronically, it is not the same thing as having real-life interactions.

One step in the right direction is to be free and flexible in your definition of belonging. Knowing that all human beings seek happiness, you can look upon them with more openness and empathy and kindness. You can work toward making yourself and others feel more included.

The longing to be connected to others still lives in us. It does not matter where—on the Internet, in your town, in your church, or across the globe—you find a social or spiritual group to be a part of. You can start with your interests and beliefs and go from there. The experience of community can be cultivated. Opportunities for making others feel included come along regularly. We can cultivate our own sense of belonging and openly include others.

Patience and Waiting

People tend to think a lot about the future, and while goals are necessary and healthy, a focus on "what's next" often causes us to miss out on the "now." Anything you can do to become less obsessed with what is going to happen next gives you more opportunity to stay in the moment. Staying in the present moment is one of the key elements of happiness. A main component of staying in the moment is patience.

Waiting is hard when you haven't learned to stay with the "now." Often, you may be thinking about the past or future or wishing that the present moment was something other than what it is. But you can change the way you feel about waiting by cultivating patience. For example, let's say your flight is delayed. Say to yourself, "My plane will leave in two hours, so I'm going to read a magazine I love." By doing so, you give yourself two hours of free time instead of two hours of waiting for your flight to leave. Taking the time to wait, being in the present, is not a waste.

Waiting is the practice of patience. Patience is the ability to wait and to listen, to go deep into stillness. Practice mindful waiting, and use any opportunity to create a sacred moment. Deep, slow breaths help you practice waiting in the present moment. Breathe in and out slowly and deeply, refreshing yourself through awareness.

Feeling that you are in the midst of an uncertain time filled with much anticipation and frustration, you may be very challenged by the practice of waiting. What better way to enjoy waiting than to sit back, treasure each moment on its own, and enjoy developing your patience.

Perception and Judgment

In practicing Right Action, you are working toward a mind free from mental constructs, a mind clear and vivid, effortless and undistracted. Without actively trying to block sense perceptions, imagination, recollections, and ruminations, you may feel uninfluenced and unmoved by them as they arise. You may remain at ease.

Your perceptions alter the vastness and serenity of your mind. Whenever thoughts arise, practice letting them undo themselves—like a ripple in a lake smoothing out. Acknowledge emotions and feelings for what they are, and allow them to pass through you like wind through the leaves of a tree. Let them be, without judging or getting caught up in them.

That little voice inside you is the product of your very active mind. Do not believe the thoughts that little voice produces. Perceptions and points of view must be examined from all angles to get a clear understanding. How many times has your mind perceived and judged a situation wrongly? Meditation is the only way to lower the rate of chatter in there. Imagine the peace you will start to experience with the growing quiet in your mind.

Present Moment

Instead of trying to think and plan everything out, dive into the present moment. The path to happiness is living each minute and hour of the day in awareness, mind and body dwelling in the present moment. Let there be no desire, and see what happens. There is no past, no future, no turmoil. You are content in the present moment. Being in the present moment is a big step toward inner peace.

Mindfulness is attending to the "now." What are all the details you can grasp right now—the sounds, sights, and feelings? Being mindful calms you and makes your mind still, like a quiet pool in the forest. All kinds of strange and wonderful "animals" will come to drink at the pool, and you will see clearly the nature of things. You will see many strange and wonderful things come and go, but you will be still. The present moment is the only place to find happiness.

Recycling and Going Green

Caring for our environment is a natural part of the Buddhist path. The Buddha encouraged us to understand more deeply the underlying unity and interconnectedness of life. If the Buddha was alive today, he'd be the living embodiment of green living. He'd be collecting cans on the freeway, riding his bike to work, and replacing all of his incandescent lightbulbs with compact fluorescents. You can take Right Action by recycling and going "green."

The term *recycling* is commonly used today to refer to the practice of using resources prudently and fully. This practice grew out of a concern for pollution, an awareness that Earth's resources are limited, and a growing respect for nature. We can recycle for all these reasons but also out of thoughtful gratitude and respect for all life.

The Buddha also taught his disciples to be careful in how they treated both animal and plant life. This care includes taking from nature only what we need, using what we need prudently, and giving something back in return. You can look into using sustainable clothing, walking or biking instead of driving, turning off unnecessary lights, giving away unneeded belongings, eating organic foods, and using renewable resources.

As we act more responsibly toward nature, the more our actions will purify and clarify our minds. Consideration of our actions and their consequences leads us to more environmentally responsible and ethical behavior.

Relationships

Relationships are a lot of work. You may see others as separate from you, and this makes it easy to judge them. But the Buddhist view that all beings are interconnected and interrelated asks us to drop the judgments and the regard of ourselves as being special and separate.

Dating and relationship problems are like any other problems: they can be solved by action. The action is not about fixing the problem, but rather about fixing yourself. If you are having a relationship problem, the other person is not the cause. You are the cause. From a Buddhist point of view, relationship is a great mirror. It is the mirror in which we see and discover ourselves. That mirror can be distorted.

In our relationships, we often misunderstand how we are connected. We may think we are two made into one, or we may think we are completely independent. There is mutual responsibility, joy, and sharing, yet, at the same time, we must understand there are also the two sides. There is not only the middle where two meet; individual space is also a necessary component of relationship.

If we try to overlap totally, we lose balance. There may be a common bond, but there are also two individual minds. We must respect that and allow the other person his or her independence. The basic principle in a relationship is sharing. We share our wisdom and knowledge and allow ourselves to be a mirror, but it's up to the individual to make personal choices.

Practicing mindfulness and awareness can help us see what's in the mirror more clearly. Mindfulness can tame the mental wildness that causes us to go off balance and help us cultivate joy and delight in loving.

Responding Rather than Reacting

To become mindful and cultivate a beginner's mind—that state before concepts, conditioning, and defenses insulate us from experiencing directly—is to see the world afresh without being lost in reactions and judgments. When seeing with clarity, you can begin to respond to the world rather than react to it. Mindfulness is loving awareness that brings a quality of compassion to your actions, speech, and thoughts. Mindfulness means choosing a response rather than simply reacting.

Our tendency is to get lost in a cycle of reactivity. In order to be able to step out of that cycle, you need to cultivate the ability to pause and recognize what is going on in the present moment. Whatever technique you use, you are working to develop skills that help you respond better during the challenges of daily living rather than reacting out of habit patterns, likes, aversions, emotions, or uncontrolled thoughts.

When you feel pain, when somebody treats you in a way that feels disrespectful, or when something goes wrong for someone you love, you feel suffering. Your mind and body go into a state of reactivity that does not help bring healing. You may blame others or yourself for what happened, bringing on more suffering. Mindfulness of this process of reactivity, developed through a meditation practice, can help you work toward cultivating pause and recognition, which should lead to a better response when you are suffering.

Think, speak, drive, text, listen, cook, eat, act, and walk more slowly. When you slow down, you'll feel more in control of your options and your inner life. From this slower place, you can see what is happening and choose how you respond rather than react.

Responsibility

Take a behavioral problem you have—like impatience or reactiveness—and look into the actions, speech, and thoughts behind it, including root causes. Taking responsibility for your actions will help you better handle your relationships, your approach to and attitude toward money, your behavior at work, and your general physical health and well-being.

Taking responsibility for your actions and the way you respond to situations in daily life is part of spiritual growth. It is really important that you understand what type of person you are and to change the unskillful behaviors you may have. Try to see yourself as others see you. You are more in control of what happens to you than you think. If you own the consequences of your behaviors, what you choose to do or not do will directly impact your happiness.

Routine

There is a lot of routine in life, and sometimes you may feel like you're on a hamster wheel. These routines seem dull and meaningless, taking time away from the activities you want to do or deem more important.

Is there something you dread doing, wondering why you have to carry out this tedious task so often? Is it getting ready for work in the morning? Is it the drive or ride to work? Paying the bills? Making meals? Why do you dread this activity so much? Is there a way to find enjoyment in the process of taking care of these burdensome and annoying routine activities?

By looking at these routines, maybe you can make changes that will alter your attitude. If something is done habitually at a certain time or in a certain way, change the routine to a ritual. A ritual is something to look forward to rather than dread. A ritual can be full of the excitement of the unknown. By taking a different route home from work, do you get to see a part of your town that you are not familiar with? Instead of using regular bread in the sandwiches you make every morning, make wraps to change things up. Small changes may make a happy difference in your perception of these mundane tasks.

We are often on autopilot during routine activities. What if you try paying attention to each action involved? For example, when washing dishes, note each step in the process: picking up a plate; the water running over it; putting soap on the dish brush; scrubbing the plate and seeing the bubbles; rinsing the plate; placing it in the dish drainer; and, finally, drying the plate with a towel and putting it in the cupboard. By placing your attention on each action, autopilot changes to actively attending to a task. The valuable skills of attention and awareness will come in very handy during those "more important" activities you plan to carry out, helping you enjoy them to the fullest.

Sexual Misconduct

Buddhism, in keeping with the principle of the Middle Way, advocates neither puritanism nor permissiveness. Sexual pleasure is not regarded as unskilled or evil, but attachment to sexual pleasure—like the love of money—is. If you can experience sexual pleasure without attachment, you are all right. But you know it is rather difficult, to put it mildly, to experience pleasure of any sort without feeling attached to it.

Sex is an expression of craving, and it is therefore relevant to try to bring it under control. One aim of spiritual practice is to bring about the cessation of craving. More importantly, if you behave recklessly and irresponsibly in sexual matters, you can cause untold harm to yourself and others. For example, people's emotions can be damaged, and unwanted children can be brought into the world. Neither of these things would happen if people didn't engage in sexual misconduct.

If you make mistakes regarding your sexual relations, recognize them and avoid repeating them. Keep in mind that sex usually involves at least one other person, so it is incumbent upon you to act responsibly and compassionately.

Shopping

Shopping is truly an addiction. People shop because of feelings of greed, desire, craving, and wanting. They are trying to fill an emptiness in their soul—a Hungry Ghost, which is a Buddhist metaphor for futile attempts to fulfill illusory desires. Shopping fills our lives with stuff and debt. To achieve the perception of happiness, you may buy more things than you need or try to buy love by purchasing things for others. Even if you can afford it, shopping is not a healthy habit for your soul.

Instead, ask yourself what it is you truly want. What needs do your temporary acquisitions fulfill for you? Is desire, greed, or discontent the cause? Do you then become consumed by the objects of your momentary desire, working hard to keep and protect them?

Consider the cravings and compulsions in your life. What do you feel you cannot live without? What price do you pay for it? What kind of fulfillment does this craving or compulsion provide? Look at the questions gently, without judging. Wait for responses to come. You can quiet your wants by acknowledging them rather than pushing them away or denying that they are there. Allow change to occur naturally.

The best exercise of all is to keep a list of what you think you want. Put the list away and then check it in a week or a month, but before checking it try to recall what is on the list. A major clue that you don't really need or want something is if you can't remember it.

Skillful Action

In practicing Buddhism, you are working to develop a state of mind called *immovable wisdom*. It means having fluidity around an unmoving center, so that your mind is clear and ready to direct its attention wherever it may be needed. No matter what circumstance lies in front of you, you want to be mindful of the situation. Mindfulness is clear comprehension, paying attention to what you are doing, and knowing whether actions are skillful or unskillful.

Anyone can become more fully engaged and involved in the experiences of daily life, cultivating "flow." The secret is attention. In the midst of working, studying, cleaning, or any other activity, stop for a moment. Be aware of where you are, and be aware of your breathing. Actively take your attention from the external world and focus it on your breath. This is a way to train your attention. You will be surprised at how much more engaged and involved in life you become by training your attention using the breath; you may be surprised by how many more skillful actions you take.

Choose a simple, regular activity that you usually do on autopilot. Resolve to make the activity a reminder to wake up your mindfulness. You could choose making tea or coffee, shaving, bathing, watering the plants, or turning on lights. Resolve to pause for a few seconds before you start the activity. Then carry out the activity with gentle and complete attention. Try to bring mindfulness to this act each time you do it.

Taking Intoxicating Substances

One of the Five Precepts of Buddhism is to abstain from intoxicating substances, which can be the basis for heedlessness. Heedlessness means moral recklessness, a disregard for the bounds between right and wrong. So, does this precept mean no drinking, no caffeine, and no drugs? Not exactly.

Abstaining means taking care to not use substances as intoxicants—as ways of soothing and distracting ourselves from the direct and intimate experience of life. In other words, whatever you use to distract yourself into heedlessness is an intoxicant. Taking medication containing alcohol, opiates, or other intoxicants for genuine medical reasons does not count, nor does eating food flavored with a small amount of liquor. Alcohol and drugs do blunt one's sense of shame and moral dread, and thus they lead almost inevitably to a breach of the other precepts.

An addict may have little hesitation to lie or steal, may lose all sense of sexual decency, and may easily be provoked to physically harm another person. Statistics confirm the connection between the use of alcohol and violent crime, traffic accidents, occupational accidents, and disharmony within the home. The problem with intoxicants is the recklessness that inevitably follows the surrendering of one's self-control. The precept of abstaining from intoxicants recognizes their addictive nature. However, it is up to you to truthfully assess how well you handle their addictive quality.

By observing this precept, you will train yourself to live more compassionately and harmoniously. This precept is a guideline for observing causes and effects in your consumption behavior and helps direct you toward the wholesome. The challenges in working with this precept are to identify any intoxicating substances you take and to deal with how you relate to them. The question of whether to abstain from alcohol entirely or to drink in moderation is an individual one that requires spiritual maturity and self-honesty.

Taking What Is Not Given

Another of the Buddha's Five Precepts is to refrain from taking that which is not freely given. One would think that refraining from stealing would be a relatively easy precept to follow, but it's not. There are more subtle forms of theft: downloading and uploading copyrighted material without permission, under-reporting cash income on one's taxes, using ideas without attribution, bringing paper clips home from the office, and inflating damage estimates for insurance reimbursement. The temptation to do petty larceny exists in the human heart.

What can you do? Pay attention; realize that not taking what is not given is about more than just respecting other people's property. For example, some of the products you buy are made with exploited labor. You could try harder to not waste natural resources, such as food and water. Are you causing more greenhouse gas emissions than necessary? Do you use recycled paper products?

Think about the ways that taking more than you need might deprive somebody else. When a winter storm is coming, many people run to the grocery store and buy enough food for a week even though they'll probably be housebound for only a few hours. Then, someone who really needs groceries finds the store shelves stripped clean. Such hoarding is exactly the kind of trouble that comes from failing to observe the precept of not taking that which is not freely given.

Thoughts

Meditation involves observing your thoughts and noting whether they are beneficial (skillful) or harmful (unskillful). Becoming more aware of the thought process is very helpful for achieving your goal of happiness. Understanding the process helps you see that you are not your thoughts; that you can give thoughts a chance to settle down and even let them go; and that you can focus on positive, loving thoughts.

You may think that what goes on in your brain is not part of your karma, but it absolutely is. There is a karmic cause and effect with your thoughts as well as with your speech and actions. Like your body, your mind needs training for optimal performance. By becoming more aware of your thought process, you are training yourself to have more control over your mind. When you have control of your mind, it can only have a positive effect on your happiness. Cultivate the ability to let a thought slip by. Don't chase after it; instead, remain an observer, and you will see right away that, overall, your actions become more skillful.

Words

Remember that how you say something is as important as what you say. Before you say anything, ask yourself whether your words will build or harm a relationship. Will your words be beneficial and skillful? And remember that how, when, and why you say things are just as important as what you say.

Consider each word carefully before you say anything, so that your speech is "right" in both form and content. Let your words be straightforward and simple. When you change what you say to Right Speech, people will recognize the change. Imagine never having to regret anything you say!

Meditations

MEDITATION FOR AWARENESS OF TIME

Note what time it is as you sit and relax, breathing deeply. Close your eyes and focus on your breath. Sit for as long as you feel comfortable. Before you open your eyes, guess the amount of time you spent in meditation. When you look at your watch or clock, you may be surprised at your underestimation. If your guess is correct, be neither pleased nor disappointed with yourself.

MEDITATION FOR BALANCE

Sit and watch the breath until you are calm. If you are right-handed, concentrate on the left side of your body, particularly your left hand and foot. Visualize yourself walking toward a door. Imagine reaching out with your left hand and turning the doorknob. (Do the opposite if you are left-handed.) In your mind, begin to walk through the doorway, being mindful of taking the first step with your left foot. As you pass through the doorway, turn toward the left and close the door with your left hand. Once you have finished the visualization, imagine powerful energy coursing up your left side. Try to bring this increased awareness of your left side into your life after the meditation.

MEDITATION ON BODY AWARENESS

Establish concentration by focusing on the breath, and then transfer your awareness to your right arm, from the fingers to the shoulder. Then do the same for the left arm. While remaining aware of your arms, become progressively conscious of your torso and then your neck, head, and face. You are now aware of your upper body. Without losing this awareness, become progressively aware of each part of the lower body. Now the whole of your physical presence is embraced. Sit in this embrace for the rest of the session. You may experience feelings of gratitude toward your body for the way it carries out its vital functions without the need for conscious control.

MEDITATION FOR COMPASSION

Sit and think about a person with whom you are struggling. Look beyond the conflict and reflect on the fact that this person is a human being like you. This person has the same desire for happiness and well-being, the same fear of suffering, and the same need for love. Note how this meditation softens your feelings.

MEDITATION FOR EMPTYING THE MIND

Stand or sit with your eyes closed and say nonsense sounds and gibberish. You can sing, shout, mumble— whatever. After twenty minutes, sit still and silent and relaxed, gathering your energy. If thoughts come, be aware of them but don't get caught up in them. Let them go.

MEDITATION ON ENOUGH

Breathe in and say, "What I have is enough." *Breathe out and think,* What I am is enough. *Breathe in and say,* "What I do is enough." *Breathe out and think,* What I have achieved is enough. *Repeat this for several minutes.*

MEDITATION FOR FEELING OVERWHELMED

Take a few seconds to relax and breathe deeply. Accept that you cannot do everything at once. You can only do one thing at a time. Focus on just one task, and clear your mind of everything else. Whenever your mind tries to think about other things still to be done, gently bring it back to the task at hand. Now focus on that one task with mindfulness. Be aware of everything about it, using all of your senses: sight, smell, touch, taste, and hearing. Calmly watch yourself doing the task until it is done. Then move on to the next task.

MEDITATION FOR GETTING UNSTUCK

Settle in. Check in with yourself and ask, How am I doing? What does not feel quite right? What do I need to pay attention to right now? Take whatever comes up and set it aside. Do this a few times until you have three or four things. Choose one thing and simply ask, What is the crux of this problem? Do not try to analyze or understand or reach a conclusion. Hold the question in awareness with simple curiosity. Wait for a revelation, which can come as a word, an image, or a feeling. Then ask, Is this right? When the answer feels right, sit with it in silence for a few moments.

MEDITATION ON A GOAL

Hold a pebble in your hand and focus your attention on it. Look at the smooth grain and the variations in hue. Feel its cool hardness on your skin. Close your eyes and squeeze the pebble in one hand. Imagine the pebble glowing in your hand, charged with energy. When you do this, you can think of a dream or goal. After the meditation, put the pebble somewhere to remind you of your goal. At any time during the day, hold the pebble in your hand and focus your mind on the dream or goal.

MEDITATION IN THE MORNING

Today, I will avoid causing harm through my physical activity; I will avoid causing harm through my speech; and I will avoid causing harm through my thoughts. Today, I will do my best to engage in beneficial physical activity; I will do my best to speak useful and pleasant words; and I will do my best to nourish well-wishing thoughts for all beings.

MEDITATION ON MOVEMENT

Breathe in and out to relax. Then move your head in whatever way seems natural. Then bring it back to rest. Do this with each body part, down to your toes. Move naturally this way and that. Then bring the body part to rest. When you are ready to end this meditation, acknowledge and appreciate your efforts.

MEDITATION TO RELAX

Bring your attention to your breathing, which should be natural. When you feel ready, repeat the word "relax" either silently or out loud. Say the first syllable "re" as you breathe in and the second syllable "lax" as you breathe out. Do not try to force your breathing into a rhythm or pattern; just keep breathing normally, matching the speed of the affirmation to your breathing. When your mind wanders, bring it back gently and continue to repeat the word "relax." Repeat this meditation for as long as feels comfortable.

MEDITATION FOR TRAVELING

Let your whole body go loose, relaxing any area of tension, and take some deep breaths. Accept that there is nothing you can do to get to your destination faster. Focus on your breathing and visualize any anxiety or worry simply floating away with each exhalation. Just let these emotions go. Each time anxiety or worry tries to come back, bring your focus back to the breath and let go. You might even want to repeat the mantra "peace" with each exhalation.

Barbara Ann Kipfer, PhD, is a lexicographer and Buddhist scholar with an MA and PhD in Buddhist Studies, an MPhil and PhD in Linguistics, and a PhD in Archaeology. She has authored more than sixty books, including the best-selling *14,000 Things to Be Happy About*, as well as *The Wish List*, *Instant Karma*, *8,789 Words of Wisdom*, *Self-Meditation*, and *What Would Buddha Say?* Visit her online at www .thingstobehappyabout.com.

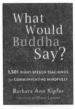